LIFE IN THE SUN
A GUIDE TO LONG-STAY HOLIDAYS & LIVING ABROAD IN RETIREMENT

LIFE IN THE SUN
A GUIDE TO LONG-STAY HOLIDAYS & LIVING ABROAD IN RETIREMENT

By Nancy Tuft

Age Concern would like to acknowledge the generous financial sponsorship provided by the TSB to allow this book to reach a wider audience than would otherwise have been possible.
A summary of the TSB's banking activities can be found on p 149.

© 1989 Nancy Tuft
Published by Age Concern England
Bernard Sunley House
60 Pitcairn Road
Mitcham
Surrey CR4 3LL

All rights reserved, no part of this work may be reproduced in any form, by mimeograph or any other means, without permission in writing from the publisher.

Editor   Claire Llewellyn
Design   Eugenie Dodd
Production   Joyce O'Shaughnessy
Illustrations   Sal Shuel
Printed by Ebenezer Baylis & Son Ltd, Worcester

ISBN 0-86242-085-7

The cover illustration has been developed from Roger Broders' poster *L'ete sur la cote d'Azur*. It has been reproduced by kind permission of PLM, Paris. We are indebted to John Murray (Publishers) Ltd for permission to reproduce *The Costa Blanca* by John Betjeman, which first appeared in his *Collected Poems*.

Although great care has been taken in the compilation of this book, Age Concern England cannot accept responsibility for any errors or omissions. The publishers strongly urge readers to take professional advice in the appropriate circumstances.

CONTENTS

Foreword 9
About the Author 10
Acknowledgements 11
Introduction 12

1 TRAVEL AND RETIREMENT: A PERFECT PARTNERSHIP

Enjoying travel in retirement 17
The travel boom for the over-50s 18
Financing your holidays 20
Don't dive in at the deep end 21

2 LONG-STAY HOLIDAYS: THE OPTIONS

Winter sun 24
Low season 25
Package holidays 26
  Hotel accommodation 28
  Self-catering apartments 29
  Packages for car drivers 30
Beyond the package 32
Rented accommodation 33
Overseas family reunions 35
Home exchange 37
Cargo-boat cruising 42

CONTENTS

Camping and caravanning 42
Voluntary work abroad 45

3 LONG-STAY HOLIDAYS: GETTING READY TO GO

Documentation 50
Passports 50
Visas 51
Financial arrangements 51
State pensions 54
Other benefits 55
Health care 56
Emergency treatment abroad 60
Travel insurance 62
Consumer protection 64
You and your car 65
Domestic arrangements 69
Your personal packing 73
Special requirements 74
On your own? 74
Disabilities 77
Older travellers 78
Second thoughts 79
Keeping in touch with home 80

CONTENTS

4 LIVING ABROAD

The right move? 84
How permanent is 'permanent'? 84
Location 84
You and your partner 86
Can you afford it? 87
Abroad is different 87
Accommodation: to rent or to buy? 89
Your property in the UK 90
Maintaining contact 92
When to return 94

Your status at home and abroad 96
Residency requirements 97
Social security and health care 99
Your tax position 101

Moving arrangements 105
Removals 105
Electrical and consumer goods 107
Pets 108
Buying a car for overseas use 109

Returning to the UK 111
An unforeseen return 111
Death abroad 112
Making a Will 113

CONTENTS

5 BUYING A PROPERTY ABROAD

A few warnings *116*

Sole ownership *120*

Defining your needs *120*
Finding a property *121*
Buying property abroad – some general guidelines *122*
Gardens abroad *126*

Other options *127*

Retirement homes and sheltered schemes *127*
Timeshare *130*

6 FURTHER INFORMATION

Useful addresses *134*

Holiday options *134*
Other sources of help and advice *136*
Consulates *139*
National Tourist Offices *140*

Recommended Reading *142*

Books and magazines *142*
Leaflets *143*

Other Publications from Age Concern *144*

About Age Concern *148*

About the TSB *149*

FOREWORD

More and more people are choosing to retire to the sun or take long holidays abroad to avoid the British winter. There are many things to consider when planning any trip overseas and with this in mind, Age Concern have produced *Life in the Sun* as a guide for anyone planning a long holiday or thinking of moving abroad permanently.

We are delighted to have helped with the publication of this extremely useful guide and look forward to advising and assisting anyone making plans for their retirement.

Peter Ellwood
Chief Executive
TSB Retail Banking

ABOUT THE AUTHOR

Nancy Tuft used to work for Central Television's *Getting On* programme for older viewers. She has researched and edited a variety of books for Age Concern England and now tutors retirement courses for the Adult Education Service in the London borough of Bromley, where she lives.

Aged 56, Nancy Tuft has three adult children and five grandchildren.

ACKNOWLEDGEMENTS

Many individuals have been involved in putting together this book. In particular I would like to thank Clifford Green and David Vessey of Allied Dunbar; Geoffrey Pilgrem of FOPDAC; Dan and Molly Lees, authors of *Travel in Retirement*; Tim Smith, Director of the Holiday Care Service and Edward McMillan Scott MEP, who first introduced me to the John Betjemen poem on page 116. Thanks are also due to Hazel Nayor, Director of Intervac GB and Vera Coppard of Travel Companions.

I should also like to acknowledge the help of Evelyn McEwen, David Bookbinder, Sally West, Sinda Lopez Fuentes and David Moncrieff, all of Age Concern England, who have worked with me on various aspects of the project. Particular thanks are due to Claire Llewellyn for her constant support and advice over the last few months.

Finally, the most heartfelt thanks of all to my own travel companion, Tony Marks.

Nancy Tuft
October 1989

INTRODUCTION

Thousands of Britons dream of moving abroad to a warmer climate on retirement. Sun-drenched days and balmy evenings have a considerably greater attraction than grey skies and cold winds for most of us. During the last few years the number of people who have chosen to turn their dream into reality has risen significantly; the number of companies eager to assist with such a move has increased proportionately.

Life in the Sun is about travel and living abroad; activities which are certainly ideally suited to the retirement years. However, the central message of the book, which runs through every chapter, is that considerable caution must be exercised before any potentially far-reaching decisions are taken. Life abroad is different; a fact which has to be accepted by anyone toying with the idea of settling overseas.

A variety of options are examined in detail, ranging from brief 'hobby' trips to long-stay holidays lasting a period of months. The weighty question of whether or not to buy a property abroad and leave the UK on a semi-permanent basis is tackled in a section of its own. The pleasures and pitfalls associated with all these alternatives are considered in a straightforward and unbiased fashion and comprehensive advice is provided on where readers can go for further information. Many people take a decision to retire abroad on the strength of nothing more than the flimsy experience gained during a succession of short summer holidays and subsequently regret their rashness at leisure. This book has been designed to ensure that its readers have a greater appreciation of the full picture before they commit themselves.

A considerable number of the arrangements which have to be made when getting ready to go are common to all lengths of stay. Planning is essential, be it in preparation for a trip lasting ten days or ten years. Topics such as ticket purchase, insurance and health are addressed in broad terms, the particular requirements associated with lengthier trips being highlighted. Other more specialised issues, among them residency permits and tax liability, are dealt with in the section on Living Abroad.

Retirement and travel are potentially a perfect partnership; the more effort and energy put into both the richer are likely to be the rewards. Nancy Tuft's book emphasises that with a little imagination and a lot of common sense life in the sun really can be idyllic, but that it is not an automatic panacea for everyone's ills.

Sally Greengross
Director
Age Concern England

1

Travel and Retirement
A Perfect Partnership

Travel is an ideal retirement hobby. At last you are free to take off – as travellers, not just tourists – and experience life in whatever setting you choose. You can opt in one season for the peace of a countryside ploughed by oxen and, in another, appreciate the sophistication and excitement of a city. Food, wine, scenery, nightlife – whatever your preference, they are all there waiting for you to seek them out.

Travelling needs planning and preparation, and planning takes time. Fortunately, in retirement, you have much more time: you can seek out new locations for holidays and research 'around' them, look up and compare routes, find out about the weather as well as keep an eye open for last-minute package bargains at your local travel agent. Not only that: now that your commitment to a job has ended, you may have the freedom to stay abroad for much longer periods of time. You can think in terms of months, if you wish, rather than weeks. Equally, if life overseas really suits you well, you can even consider living there for a number of years.

Going by the principle that the more effort you put into a venture, the greater the rewards, holidays in retirement should be much more leisurely and enjoyable than the snatched couple of weeks when you were working. When people are in full-time work there is often a tendency to 'play safe' with holidays in order to avoid disappointment. The fortnight's break is a well-earned, much-needed escape, and because this free time is so highly-prized, a lot is at stake. Risks are to be avoided at all costs.

In retirement, your priorities are likely to change. Escape isn't necessarily so much of an issue, nor is rest and relaxation. Change and stimulus may be the missing factors in life, so holidays now can be rather more adventurous; not climbing Everest or exploring the Amazon, but perhaps a barge trip along the canals of Brittany or Burgundy, or an Alpine walking tour. You can afford to experiment a little more, trying new and different types of holiday (new and different to *you*, that is). Touring with your car on the Continent, taking your time and appreciating good food and scenery on the way, may be an enjoyable and relaxing first-time experience for you; you don't know the benefits until you try it. If for some reason your fishing or camping trip doesn't work out as well as expected, you haven't wasted your precious quota of leave and you don't have to wait until next year to try again at something else.

As a retired holidaymaker you don't have to consider anyone else, other than your partner (or accompanying friend) of course, and even then you may choose to go your separate ways on hobby holidays. No longer do you have to worry about a safe beach where the children can play, or choose a resort where teenagers won't be bored in the evenings. Holidays need no longer be centred around the swimming pool. Best of all, you don't have to get back to the office for Monday morning.

Enjoying travel in retirement

Holidays are good for you! Initially, they provide something special to look forward to, optimistic entries on the calendar which brighten up the dull days and help to keep depression at bay. You are more likely to feel positive about life when you have on-going incentives, such as travel plans, to work on. When you are actually on holiday, you will probably spend much more time outdoors, in the fresh air. You may take more exercise without even noticing the extra effort. You should feel better as a result.

All the practical arrangements that are needed when planning an extended trip will keep you active and busy in the months before you travel. There will be many things to sort out: working out the best routes, finding detailed maps and checking timetables. This all adds to the challenge of adapting to an unfamiliar environment for a month or so.

Preparation for survival abroad is likely to lead you to new areas of interest. You will probably need to brush up your knowledge of the language of your chosen country. Learning a foreign language is often an activity you *intend* to do, but which you never quite get round to actually *doing*. A fortnight's holiday in a country is never much of an incentive, but the prospect of lengthy stays in the future should spur you on. Having successfully reached a basic standard, you then have the added encouragement to become more fluent. Equally, an impending touring holiday in your car might provide the impetus to take car maintenance lessons or a course in first aid.

These new areas of interest don't need to end with your holiday. When you come home, you may well question whether you really are making the most of the free time that retirement brings. Are you maximising your potential regarding health and hobbies? A successful holiday can spark off or revive an interest in a particular sport – keep fit, perhaps, or swimming. You may want to learn more about French, Italian or Portuguese cookery. A wish to sustain the memory of a special trip abroad can be the start of new and absorbing activities: photography, painting or writing. Few people ever think of sound recording as a means of recapturing local atmosphere; how about learning more about video-making for your next trip?

The travel boom for the over-50s

Once you are retired, you have two important advantages as a traveller: you have the freedom and flexibility to travel at off-peak times, and you can stay away for longer periods. These two factors have proved to be the travel industry's heaven-sent answer to the problem of 'seasonality'. Hence the great boom in travel for the over-50s. Planes and hotels can be kept full and busy all year round, which means regular employment, a boost in profits, and the ability to keep down costs.

The comparatively low price of long-stay holidays results from the way these 'packages' are costed. The fixed item in the cost of any holiday abroad is the flight charge, which is as much for seven days as for seventy. Accommodation charges drop proportionally week by week the longer the stay. Saga was the pioneer and still is brand leader in travel for the older age group, but now most major tour operators have subsidiary companies or off-shoots providing package holidays especially for the over-50s.

The travel boom for the over-50s has brought with it a number of advantages for the consumer. It has enabled huge numbers of people to experience foreign travel for the first time, and at a price they can afford. But, of course, there have been some drawbacks. The tour operators, with their cheap winter-sun packages, have been slow to see retired people as individuals with widely differing tastes. Young company 'reps' need to be educated to reject ageist and outdated stereotypes which can get in the way of providing suitable services for younger and more sophisticated retired people. A former teacher identified this problem in the following account of his Alpine walking holiday.

> 'There we were, a nice group of like-minded people, enjoying the scenery which was breathtaking, and the flowers and each other's company. And here was this young rep jollying us along trying to get us all to sing "This old man" – you know, the "Knick-knack-paddywhack, give-a-dog-a-bone" song.
>
> 'We were all there because we liked walking; we didn't need anything else. We didn't want to hurt her feelings – she was trying hard and she meant well. But in the end, one of us had to take her on one side and explain we were quite happy without the singing. It could have ruined the holiday.'

Of course companionship is important for retired people on holiday, particularly for those who live alone, but it can develop naturally and spontaneously, given the right setting.

Another automatic and questionable assumption that tour operators make is that customers want and expect more and more luxury travel. This is not necessarily the case. Holidaymakers usually expect something different, but different does not have to mean more luxurious, or even a more distant destination. It can mean being more selective and imaginative, providing travellers with opportunities to stretch themselves, physically and mentally – challenges which can be lacking in retirement.

Most customers, of course, don't always know what they want until someone provides it. 'Consumers are historians, not clairvoyants; they are conditioned by what they already know, not what might be', comments Eric Midwinter, General Secretary of the University of the Third Age – U3A (see p 135). U3A has started to develop special interest trips abroad for member groups that are interested in topics such as European art and architecture. There is enormous potential in group travel, organised by retired people themselves, using the facilities of a small travel agency or tour operator, of the kind which already specialise in tailor-made special interest holidays. Many of these small firms advertise holidays in U3A's newspaper, *The Third Age*, as well as in specialist publications; for example, botanical tours in the journal of the Royal Horticultural Society and birdwatching trips in the magazine of the Royal Society for the Protection of Birds.

Long-stay holidays can offer a new dimension to retirement, providing a choice of second chances as well as new opportunities. Today a whole range of student travel experiences are taken for granted by the young, but these were unavailable between the war years and, indeed, for some time after that. Exchanges, language study courses abroad, *en famille* arrangements are all practical introductions to another country and its people, as well as opportunites to improve language skills (see p 134). If you missed out on those experiences at the time, it's not too late to catch up.

Financing your holidays

While travel and retirement complement each other perfectly, travel and a pension may not. During your working life you probably had spare income but not sufficient time to spend it on holidays. In retirement, it is often the other way round; more time and less cash.

One way to finance further trips could be a part-time job, temporary or otherwise. Now that the earnings rule has been abolished, there is no financial disincentive to have a job, perhaps in the high summer holiday season or the busy pre-Christmas or sales period. This odd-jobbing is a means of keeping in touch with the world of work, and it can be a psychological boost to mix with other generations. But that's not all: the money you earn is a welcome contribution to the quality of life . . . and towards the next trip!

Another means of financing a holiday is perhaps by the judicious letting of a room in your house to a student. A foreign student could provide you with language practice as well as additional earnings.

Don't dive in at the deep end

When you first retire, you need to give yourself several months of acclimatisation in your own home before you begin thinking about long periods abroad. Retirement has its own impact and you will need time to adapt to your new lifestyle. Asking yourself to make two different kinds of adaptation simultaneously – retirement *and* life abroad – might be overwhelming.

After this period of adaptation, however, you can experiment with overseas travel to your heart's content. You can start off cautiously with a short package holiday before plunging in deeper. The more you gain in confidence, the longer you may choose to stay.

As well as holidays in the sun, retirement presents the exciting possibility of living abroad on a more or less permanent basis. Before launching into this, you would be wise to try out several long-stay self-catering holidays first. Even if you do finally decide to go and live abroad you may find a UK base a very reassuring place to come back to.

A sensible compromise for many people is the long-stay holiday, combining a few months of life abroad with all the comforts and familiarity of home. The next chapter discusses the options for long-stay holidays, and reveals why they can be the very best of both worlds!

2

Long-Stay Holidays
The Options

Long-stay holidays are best taken at a time when the rest of the world is at home and at work. Why put up with the crowds when they can be avoided, or pay peak-season prices when you don't have to? If you are retired you now have the freedom to buy more for your money. The two options open to you in terms of the timing of your holiday are either the winter months or the low season.

Winter sun

Most people feel better for a bit of sunshine. A winter-sun holiday destination, where you can sit outside at a pavement cafe, enjoying a coffee or a drink in the open air, feeling the warmth of the sun soaking into your skin and watching the rest of the world go by can be as little as two hours' flying time away. All this is a tonic in itself. What's more, its soothing, quick-acting effect can start working the moment you step off the plane and feel that first gentle warm air all around you. Instinctively, you seem to relax and let your cares and worries fade into insignificance.

A successful winter-sun holiday can be a bigger psychological boost than a summer break; the contrast with the British winter is so enormous. A frequent and common topic of cafe conversation among winter holidaymakers is the awful weather back home. This seems to draw strangers together, without any need for formal introductions. Cafe encounters themselves, with their easy table-to-table informality, are a refreshing contrast to life back home where the natural tendency for many retired people most winter afternoons is to make a cup of tea, draw the curtains to shut out the grey skies and switch on the radio or television. This can add up to a sluggish state of semi-hibernation, and it is easy to put on weight and become unfit through inactivity and inertia.

For many people, migration to a sunnier climate is an attractive alternative. Spending the worst months of the winter abroad may be a sensible step, particularly if you suffer from something like a rheumatic or respiratory complaint. But you don't have to suffer ill health to feel the benefits. A lot of healthy people who go on a winter-sun holiday are likely to come home feeling brighter, fitter and, possibly, slimmer. There is every encouragement to remain active and enjoy a range of sports not always easily available, affordable or accessible in the UK. Tennis courts, swimming pools and golf courses may be close at hand, and they can act as an incentive to revive forgotten sporting skills. Coaching is often included in your 'package', and there are chances to learn and try new activities.

People in a holiday mood, away from the restraints of home, will often be tempted to have a go at something different. Seeing someone your own age, floundering about enjoying themselves in the swimming pool is a great inhibition chaser. They're obviously having a great time: why shouldn't you? A luxury hotel pool is a much more attractive proposition than the local swimming baths at home, and a daily swim is a good habit to acquire. Similarly, if you are able to attend the keep-fit classes, you may well feel the benefit after only a couple of weeks.

A winter-sun holiday can be part of many people's general get-yourself-fit programme. After all, the sun is the great giver of energy and a source of revitalisation. Wouldn't it be good to get away, and come home, not only with a healthy glow on your skin, but also a few kilos lighter – and having met lots of new people and seen new places?

Low season

The so-called 'low season' in Europe falls in April, May, September and October. These are good months for long-stay holidaymakers, particularly for those who like exploring new places. Touring and sightseeing in spring or autumn is often much more comfortable and enjoyable than in the oppressive heat of high summer, an important consideration for both car drivers and their passengers. Yet you will still enjoy appreciably better weather than back home: a warm, early spring or some golden late-summer days.

These months are the ideal time to plan a cooler, more leisurely trip back to some of those places which perhaps attracted your interest on previous summer holidays. Have you ever said 'I'd love to come back again and spend more time here one day...'? Many a pleasant evening can be spent down 'Memory Lane', reminiscing over old photographs and recalling past trips, while you finalise plans for a less-pressurised return visit, out of the heat of the sun and at a time when every museum and cathedral isn't packed with groups of tourists.

Travelling in low season has many advantages: the roads are less busy, so are the ferries; there is less likelihood of airport delays; accommodation is cheaper and rarely has to be booked in advance. This time round, you may decide to take your car, or use local car hire, in order to have greater freedom and flexibility.

The low-season months are generally still warm enough for outdoor activities such as walking, cycling, camping, caravanning or canal cruising. But it is a matter of always matching the location and the time of year to the kind of holiday you want. Whatever the holiday, outdoor-based, hotel package or otherwise, it is vital that you enquire at the national tourist office (see p 140) what the local weather conditions are likely to be in that spot at that time of year. Travel brochures will not always provide detailed information about regional variations, those quirky combinations of warm sun and keen winds, as well as rain patterns. Proximity to the sea or mountains can make a big difference – temperatures can be quite chilly in the evenings, compared with the days. Macs, umbrellas, cardigans and sweaters should certainly be part of your luggage.

Package holidays

If your experience of overseas travel has generally been limited to a short-stay annual package holiday abroad, then perhaps a long-stay package holiday would be the wisest first step if you are considering moving away from home on a more permanent basis. All your travel and accommodation arrangements are then taken care of by your tour operator. As you gain in confidence, you may eventually wish to venture 'beyond the package' and arrange your itinerary personally, tailoring destinations and accommodation to your own tastes and needs.

The principal tour operators, whose brochures are available in all High Street travel agents, include Thomson, Cosmos, Intasun, Horizon and Falcon. (Saga and Portland do not use travel agents; you deal with them direct. See p 135.) Prospective holidaymakers can choose either residential hotel accommodation or self-catering apartments in a variety of resorts. Winter-sun packages are available between November and April and proposed periods of stay are anything from seven to eighty-four nights, occasionally longer. Some incorporate the Christmas break, others are arranged on either side.

The Algarve, the Costa Blanca, the Costa del Sol, Cyprus, Gran Canaria, Madeira, Majorca, Malta and Tenerife, among others, are well represented by all the companies. When you come to choose your holiday location, remember that popular seaside resorts like these are given a significance in the holiday brochures out of all proportion to their standing in the region, compared with other, older towns and cities. Resorts are often just former fishing villages, usually within reach of somewhere with more historic and cultural connections: Benidorm, for example, is near Valencia and Alicante; Torremolinos is within easy reach of Malaga and Granada. Information gathered from the national tourist office will indicate what is feasible in the way of day trips.

The more you can find out about an area beforehand, the more successful your ultimate choice of holiday destination will be. Good planning gives you a headstart once you are on holiday, and the research can often be done more easily in this country before you leave than actually 'on the ground'. High Street bookshops stock an impressive range of guidebooks these days, and you can borrow or order travel books from your local public library. The library may also keep issues of *Holiday Which?* (see p 142). These contain not only articles on individual resorts around the world, but also sound information and advice on all aspects of holiday travel. Make a point, too, of catching the various holiday programmes on radio and television. All these sources can add to your awareness of what different locations have to offer.

Whichever location you choose for your package holiday, and whether it's in a hotel or a self-catering apartment, keep a close eye on the detail. You will obviously compare the costs of different holidays carefully, but notice, too, the times of flights and the airports of departure. A flight from your local airport at a reasonable hour is not only wonderfully convenient, it can make quite a difference to costs, especially if the alternative is an overnight stay in a London hotel in order to catch an early flight next morning.

Another vital point of detail is whether the hotel or apartment is suitable for your needs. Some brochures give a company telephone number where people with limited mobility can check on the suitability or otherwise of the accommodation on offer. Some overseas hotels may have awkward steps at the entrance of the hotel, or outside the dining room; or baths with high sides which are difficult to step in and out of. Further advice for disabled travellers is given later in the book (see p 77).

HOTEL ACCOMMODATION

On long-stay package holidays, the usual hotel terms apply: half board or full board, waiter or buffet service. Single-room supplements vary according to the date of your holiday.

An important feature of some of these holidays is a substantial entertainment programme. Some company reps place great emphasis on creating a friendly, sociable club-type atmosphere. First-timers abroad are well looked after and there is sometimes an introductory 'walkabout' around the area, so that they can familiarise themselves with the vicinity of the hotel. Ballroom and sequence dancing may be popular evening entertainment. Competitions for the most charming couple or the most elegant grandfather might not be to everyone's taste, but they are not compulsory! A random selection of daytime activities includes whist, bridge, foreign cookery classes, language lessons, flower arranging and cocktail demonstrations, all of which may be welcome diversions on a rainy day. There are also the usual accompanied excursions to local places of interest.

More experienced travellers, who prefer to explore the locality independently, can go off sightseeing on their own to visit museums, galleries and churches and to investigate the local shops. Your hotel can be just the base from which you set out on your own adventures, in your hired car or on local buses or trains. However, even in popular resorts, street lighting may not be up to British standards, so everyone should be cautious when walking around quiet streets after dark. Older tourists, in particular, may be vulnerable to being robbed, even within a short distance of the hotel. There has been an increase in petty crime in most places in recent years. Much of it tends to be opportunist, so you would be well advised to avoid wearing valuable jewellery or carrying too much cash around.

On long-stay holidays there are some additional facilities not normally found on brief hotel package holidays. One feature offered by both Saga and Thomson's Young at Heart holidays is a non-denominational church service, usually in a room in the hotel, led by a chaplain who is resident and easily available to anyone wanting a quiet chat. At some hotels a regular health clinic is held, with a nurse and/or doctor in attendance. This can be reassuring for anyone who has had recent health worries, such as a heart attack or stroke (see Special Requirements p 74).

SELF-CATERING APARTMENTS

All the tour operators offer the option of self-catering apartments, but it has to be said that there is not a great deal of saving in the price. Prices tend to be based on an occupancy of four people to a one-bedroom apartment (with a convertible bed in the lounge), so be on your guard against 'under-occupancy supplements' according to dates. Studio apartments (ie one room only) are also available. A cleaning service is included in the price, and towels and linen are changed once or twice a week. Cooking facilities are usually fairly basic in these apartments, with just a couple of rings and a grill.

Apartments are usually located in high-rise blocks with lifts. Supermarkets, shops, vegetable markets and restaurants are often near by. Facilities on the site vary. There is usually a cafeteria or restaurant, sometimes a swimming pool and maybe a shop. There may be a bar or a communal lounge with a video, but tenants are unlikely to enjoy the range of entertainment provided for hotel residents. Your own supply of paperbacks, playing cards and games like 'Scrabble' could come in useful.

PACKAGES FOR CAR DRIVERS

Having a car at your disposal means there is a far greater range of self-catering holiday homes available to you to rent in the country or on the coast. Much of this accommodation is available outside the peak season, and at much lower rates. Many companies which let villas, farmhouses and cottages offer the holidaymaker a complete package, comprising the rented accomodation *and* travel arrangements.

France is an obvious choice for car drivers who do not want to travel a long way. The *Gîtes de France Handbook* (see p 134) offers a choice of 2000 rural 'gites'. These are country lets in farmhouses, converted barns or, perhaps, a self-contained flat in the house of the owner, often a local farmer. Gites are listed in the handbook by region and department of France with a classification symbol intended as a guide to standards and facilities. Gites do not aim to compete with hotels; you take your own linen and are expected to leave the place clean and tidy when you depart. Travel bookings are in conjunction with P&O European Car Ferries. There are various companies which specialise in self-catering packages for car drivers, details of which are often carried in the quality Sunday Press.

Much of the country accommodation offered by these companies is in old stone buildings lovingly restored by their owners. Many will sleep up to six or eight people. This raises the possibility of a joint holiday, sharing the car and accommodation with like-minded friends. Going on holiday with friends does cut costs and can be fun (the extra companionship might be especially welcome on a long-stay holiday in a quiet area), but it also needs a strong commitment on everyone's part to make it a success. You would also have to agree on a few 'house rules' about sharing out the cooking and cleaning. A trial run together on a short break, in order to test compatability, might be a good idea prior to a long-stay arrangement.

Sharing or not, the choice of location is important for a long stay and you will need to have done some research before finally deciding on a particular area. Getting away from it all for a couple of weeks in a rural retreat is one thing; many people welcome a fortnight of peace and solitude. A longer stay is quite a different proposition and might not work so well if your house were too remote or not near to restaurants and shops; or if it rained a lot and you were kept indoors. So read the brochure descriptions of properties carefully, with a long stay in mind; they are individually written and are generally fairly detailed, but you can always ask the company about anything you are unsure of. You will need to check on the provision, and extra cost, of heating – particularly in Northern Europe. For a long stay, you will also need to know what laundry facilities there are.

Self-catering abroad is quite a challenge in self-reliance, especially in the country, where locals are not necessarily used to tourists. Holidays like this in France or elsewhere will appeal to those who appreciate good food and wine and who are tempted by the idea of fetching fresh croissants for breakfast each morning from the village bakery. Shopping and cooking are integral parts of this sort of holiday and visits to the village shops and vegetable markets provide some of the first authentic opportunities to practise the language. If this kind of holiday suits you, then you cannot help but feel the benefits after a month or so. You will hopefully have a different and challenging holiday in a beautiful part of the world and your language skills will probably improve considerably.

Beyond the package

There are so many variations on package holidays now; even nomadic-type holidays like canal cruising, camping and caravanning come in packages. This can save a lot of headaches if you are trying something new abroad for the first time and do not want to be bothered with fixing separate holiday and travel bookings. Packages are fine when what is being packaged is a bargain; either the price is right or the convenience saves you unnecessary trouble. What many holidaymakers with a bit of experience do *not* like is when they feel that it is *they* who are being packaged. An obvious example of this is being addressed as part of a group, when you would rather identify yourself as an individual. Some holidaymakers prefer to avoid the tourist label and choose to make their own arrangements.

The joy of handling your own holiday arrangements is that you can tailor most of the details to your own taste. You can stay way off the tourist track, perhaps in a mountain village which you just chanced upon once, or which was warmly recommended by a like-minded friend. Another advantage is the flexibility. If you are having a marvellous time and want to extend your stay, then you can do so. Plans can change; you don't *have* to travel on pre-arranged dates. Conversely, if some part of the arrangement hasn't worked out, you have the freedom to improve things by moving on to different accommodation or a different place.

You can enjoy a long stay abroad as part of a couple, with a friend or on your own. Being an independent traveller is fine, provided you don't lose out financially. Everyone needs to shop around for the best bargains in both travel and accommodation. The Air Travel Advisory Bureau (see p 136) is a telephone information service telling you which travel agents are offering genuinely discounted flights; they can also supply information on travel within most countries. (Beware of cut price flights offered by anyone without an ATOL licence – see p 65). Something to look forward to is a European Community (EC) Over-60s Card, which may be introduced in 1991 or soon after, entitling the bearer to concessions on transport, tourism and leisure on the same basis as pensioners who are nationals of that country.

Ideas for finding attractive accommodation, and at a reasonable price, are given in the following pages. Some of the options may sound more demanding than others, but this is probably only because you have never tried them. Remember: there is always a first time for everyone.

RENTED ACCOMMODATION

You may feel that there is little point in going to the trouble of finding your own rented accommodation and then fixing up travel arrangements, when certain companies will do it for you. But there are some advantages. As with all holidays that you arrange for yourself, you can plan for everything to be just as you would like it. But in addition, if you look through the brochures of rented accommodation on offer in the packages, you will notice that very few of the properties are in towns or cities; they tend to be unevenly distributed throughout the country, and are mainly on the coast or in rural areas. If you take care of your own arrangements, you will be able to find accommodation in the very place that you want to stay – perhaps in the old part of a well-placed and interesting town or city.

Finding your own holiday accommodation to rent is ideally done on the spot, in advance of your main trip. Not only can you inspect the accommodation, but you can also gain first-hand knowledge of facilities such as shops, restaurants, medical care and local transport. A short package holiday (your own, or that of an interested and willing friend or relative) is a useful way to check out the possibilities for another, more extended stay in the same part of the country. Another possibility if you are a car driver is to stop off and explore an area you are interested in while en route to another destination.

Whichever way you choose to conduct your research, one of the first places to head for is the local tourist information centre. Most towns will have such an office which should be able to supply you with lists of the accommodation available in the area, usually with some grading system for easy reference. You should also be able to obtain details of the low-season rates from the same source. It may not always be possible to get this very localised information from the national tourist office in the UK.

In addition to finding the right location and comfortable accommodation for your stay, you will also have to plan your travel arrangements. An early decision will be whether or not to take your car, if you have one. Obviously, the more remote your accommodation is – and this may be its very appeal – the more you will need a car for everyday transport and for sightseeing. Conversely, in a large town or city you may be able to do without one. Most of the larger travel agents should be able to supply information on the different costs of crossings by car ferry, as well as on flydrive (flight plus car hire). This will enable you to make financial comparisons and, taking into account other relevant information – such as personal preferences, the projected mileage, fuel costs, the amount you intend using the car and the local transport facilities – you will be able to make an informed decision.

Renting unseen from the UK is a less satisfactory alternative for a long stay, although there are a couple of agencies that can help. Property lets in a wide range of countries including Spain, Portugal, Italy, Belgium, Switzerland and Austria are listed in a brochure from Interhome (see p 135). Many of their lets are suitable for two people, but there are plenty that will accommodate more, so sharing with friends is a possibility (see p 31). Their low season is from April to June and from September to November. As with all holiday property lets, there are often bargain weeks to be had at short notice. Although Interhome take care of the accommodation, it is still up to you to make your own travel arrangements of course.

AA Travel run a European Property Register (see p 136) which consists of villas and apartments, owned by UK residents who use them as second homes for part of the year but who want to let them for the remaining period. For a small fee, AA Travel will send details of at least 15 properties which fit your requirements, along with the name and telephone numbers of their owners. The properties are not inspected and you have to negotiate the rent direct with the owner, but the AA do offer free third-party insurance to cover any major accidental damage.

OVERSEAS FAMILY REUNIONS

The earliest kind of long-stay holiday abroad that people used to undertake in retirement was probably the overseas reunion trip, visiting younger relatives who had settled in 'new world' countries. The first reunion trips were low-cost sea voyages in the 1950s for the parents of war brides. Friendship clubs, such as CANUSPA (Canada, Australia, New Zealand and United States Parents and Associates – see p 134) still exist and they offer members escort and other services on long-haul flights. Seasoned travellers frequently continue to take these long trips until well into their 80s and 90s; there are useful tips for elderly passengers in the section on Special Requirements (see p 74).

Lion World Travel (see p 135) run four longstanding clubs: Friends of the Koala (Australia), Kiwi (New Zealand), Springbok (South Africa) and Canada/United States Associations. Membership benefits include 'no age limit/no medicals' travel insurance, escorted flights and stopovers.

Now that faraway places like Canada, Australia and South Africa have become holiday destinations in their own right, it is possible to combine a family visit with an independent holiday spent sightseeing elsewhere in the country. Lion World Travel will help you arrange this kind of combination, as will Saga (see p 135). Saga's Fare Deal flights cover the United States, Canada, Australia,

New Zealand, South Africa and Zimbabwe, and you can pre-book air travel and car hire within most of these countries at special discount rates.

To make your trip a real success, do agree plans with your relatives well in advance. It is vital that you all discuss and agree on the length of your stay before deciding on dates. Your relatives will be the best people to advise on the most pleasant time of year for a visit to their region. For example, in the United States, the summer can be uncomfortably hot, while autumn can be short; the 'fall', with its sudden drop in temperature, happens virtually overnight. Our autumn is a good time to visit Australia and New Zealand because, of course, this is their spring. Christmas in Australia is in the full heat of summer and therefore perhaps, not such a good time to go. It is worth remembering that Christmas is a very busy time for airlines, and flights anywhere need to be booked well in advance.

Even if you are not planning an additional holiday alongside your reunion trip, you can always do some local sightseeing independently. If you are part of a couple, you already have a companion. If you are on your own, it may be possible to meet others in your age group to accompany you on day trips. Local introductions can possibly be arranged through a seniors club, or church-based group or just on a neighbourhood basis. Your relatives may be delighted to follow up contacts on your behalf, especially if the initial suggestion comes from you. The most popular house guests are generally those who don't need constant entertaining and who don't mind being left to their own devices for some of the time. One of the problems of a long-stay visit is that other members of the family are not on vacation and have their own lives to lead. This probably means a full-time commitment to job or school, as well as a social life – playing sports or seeing friends. Arranging a few trips for yourself may give your family a pleasant break from their role as hosts, and – in the long term – may make the rest of your stay with them all the more enjoyable.

Occasionally, a much longed-for reunion trip does not live up to expectations, often for no other reason than too much was expected from it in the first place. The intensity of a long visit, especially after a considerable period of separation, can be a difficult adjustment to make. It is a sad truth that family ties sometimes survive better at a distance. The bond between you and a child living abroad may still be strong, but your child's loyalties are bound to be divided between you and their immediate family. Growing grandchildren, absorbed in their own activities, can sometimes seem very offhand, but this applies equally to grandchildren at home. If they live halfway around the world from you, then you are likely to be a comparative stranger in their home.

It may take an extra special effort on your part to make the visit a success. Why not buy the occasional bottle of wine? Or treat everyone to a meal at a local restaurant or pancake house? Or pay for a special day out? All these are ways of showing you want to reciprocate in some way and make a positive contribution to your stay. You can also publicise the fact that when the grandchildren are old enough to visit the UK, they will always be welcome to stay.

It may be that your reunion is a trial run, while you are deciding whether or not to make a more permanent move to your family's country of residence. The crucial question to ask yourself is: would you be considering this step for any other reason than to be nearer to the family? How would you feel, for example, if your son or daughter had a subsequent job move to the other side of the country and you were left behind? Would you feel stranded? Do you like the country enough for its own sake? You need to get the feel of independent life there, if you can, for a period of at least a year before committing yourself to such a big change. The issue of living abroad is discussed in greater detail in Chapter 4.

HOME EXCHANGE

It can be ironic that whereas when you were working you may have had spare income but insufficient time for holidays, in retirement you are likely to have more time but less cash. Don't let this stop you travelling before you have looked closely at some practical solutions.

One such solution is temporary home-swapping with someone abroad who can fit in with your plans. You live in their home for an agreed period of time, while they live in yours. It is an arrangement based on mutual trust and goodwill. There are well-established agencies who specialise in making suitable introductions and in producing regular directories which list people who are looking for home exchanges. There is a fee involved, but if you are a first timer, it may be a good idea to take advantage of the years of experience that some of these agencies have clocked up.

One of the major home-exchange organisations is Intervac, (see p 135) which began in 1953. Intervac is now developing the idea of a special section within its directories that will deal specifically with retired people able to negotiate longer periods than the average two to four weeks, and who want to do this all year round, not just in July and August.

Other home-swappers make arrangements through personal contacts only: friends of friends, or fellow members of clubs or social organisations such as Rotary, the Women's Institute or retirement groups. A professional journal or newsletter can be another means of contacting like-minded people in other countries. Many regular home-swappers share similar professional backgrounds: clergymen, teachers, lecturers and health workers.

The first stage in the preparation for a home exchange is deciding how best to present your home and the surrounding area as an interesting and attractive proposition to a prospective visitor from abroad. A normal entry in a home-exchange directory will consist of a list of basic abbreviations to describe your home, but – for a small extra payment – a photograph or illustration can be printed which will lend an attractive touch of individuality to your entry.

The second stage in the preparation is compiling and photocopying detailed information about your area to send to prospective visitors in the early stages of their enquiries. Your town or city may already be on the tourist map, in which case you can probably obtain leaflets about local museums, historic buildings and other attractions from the tourist department in the town hall. Another good source for this kind of publicity material is your local public library. Remember to gather leaflets about sports facilities – tennis courts, golf clubs and swimming baths. Where are the nearest theatres and cinemas? Is there a good shopping centre within reach? Does your local pub serve real ale? Is there an interesting local factory which organises visits? Is there a summer arts festival? Your local horticultural society's annual exhibition might not come up to Chelsea standard, but it may well be of interest to a foreign visitor.

Once you have made contact with a prospective exchanger, you can find out their particular interests and hobbies and match these up with local events. In fact, the better you get to know your house-swap partners via letters and phone calls, the simpler it will be to make the following practical arrangements.

◆ Sort out beforehand who pays the gas, electricity and telephone bills during the period of the exchange. What is the understanding about food in the freezer?

◆ Check carefully with your insurance company the situation regarding house contents while visitors are living in your house. Check the insurance position if you are also exchanging cars. Are you covered for holiday cancellation in the event of illness or emergency?

◆ Leave vital domestic information such as *simple* instructions on how appliances work. (The language of the instruction booklets will probably be too complex for foreign visitors.) Explain where the fuse box is.

◆ Provide simple transport information such as bus and train timetables, and the card of a local minicab service. Leave a local street map showing your home in relation to shops, station, bus stops, etc.

◆ Leave emergency phone numbers for a plumber, electrician and doctor. Do you have a friendly neighbour who is willing to drop in and make sure all is well and be 'on call' in case of difficulty?

◆ Store precious breakables in the loft. Lock away anything you wish to remain undisturbed.

♦ Leave guests as much wardrobe and drawer space as you would expect yourself.

This may sound like a lot of work, but happy home-swappers say there is nothing like an impending exchange to spur you into action; spring-cleaning, jumble-sale sort outs and longstanding DIY repairs all seem to get done in time. The fact that successful exchangers repeat the experience again and again, is sufficient evidence that it can and does work well for many. Remember, if you would like to try the arrangement out to see how it suits you before committing yourself to a long-stay trip abroad, you could always try a one- or two-week exchange within the UK first; Cornwall may not seem as daunting as California!

If you are willing to put in the time it takes to prepare for a home exchange, then this kind of holiday has lots of advantages.

♦ There are no hotel bills or rent to pay, so what you save on accommodation will often 'pay' for the holiday, or will enable you to spend more – and go further – on your journey.

♦ You can agree to exchange not only your house but your car too, subject to satisfactory insurance arrangements. This saves you petrol and ferry charges or the cost of car hire, and gives you the flexibility of your own transport, which – in other circumstances – you might have gone without.

♦ You have a much wider choice of unusual locations, well off the usual tourist map. But you must be willing to be flexible and ready to compromise.

♦ You are likely to have the privacy of a roomy, comfortable base with all the facilities of home: washing machine, fridge, cooker, phone, telelvision, etc.

♦ Reciprocal arrangements are possible regarding the feeding of pets, which will save cattery or kennel fees. Similarly, houseplants and gardens can be watered, and the grass can be cut, providing all this is agreed beforehand.

♦ Contact with the neighbours and friends of your house-swap partners can lead to invitations to neighbourhood activities: barbecues, college baseball games, dances, etc. These opportunities to share the everyday lives of people in other countries are rarely available to tourists on package holidays.

── ***Sheila Clarke*** is a retired teacher who lives in Cambridge, and she has completed around 57 home exchanges, with visitors from as far afield as Lapland and Tasmania. Ten years ago, after the death of her husband, Sheila never expected to exchange homes again. She felt she couldn't do it alone. But she did. Her experiences have since included a stay in a ranch house in the Australian outback, where possums sat on her roof in the morning, kangaroos loped past in the afternoon, and jackasses laughed at dawn and dusk. Sheila saw her first reindeer in Lapland and has watched the sun rise at three in the morning over a Norwegian fjord. In Finland she stayed by a lake where she woke in the morning to the sound of fish 'plopping' in and out of the water.

Sheila has now exchanged houses many times since the death of her husband – both in this country and abroad – developing a worldwide network of friendships which have flourished with the years. 'I'm not a millionaire,' she says, 'just a retired teacher with a liking for travel. I couldn't possibly afford to stay in hotels in all the places I've been to!' Last year Sheila went to Spain via an Intervac introduction to Madrid, and this year she has booked an exchange in Alaska.

Intervac and Home Interchange (see p 135) publish regularly updated directories which cover a wide variety of countries. These directories are prepared well in advance, so you need to keep a close eye on the deadlines for entries. An initial enquiry will provide you with all the information you need regarding fees, the layout of the directories, how to prepare your entry and the various deadlines throughout the year. Each company gives full guidelines for making contact with prospective home-swappers. Both these agencies can also offer other options, such as exchange hospitality, on a reciprocal guest arrangement.

Global Home Exchange (see p 134) specialise in exchanges with the United States. This agency does not publish a directory. It charges a membership fee, operates an inspection service and will try to arrange a suitable match for you. There is an additional fee for a successfully completed exchange.

CARGO-BOAT CRUISING

Leisurely travel on a passenger-carrying cargo vessel can be a real adventure. It can be cheaper, more interesting and more exciting than the conventional package-holiday cruise. Such vessels can only accommodate a few passengers, so you won't find the range of entertainment on board that you associate with a luxury passenger cruise; there are no ballrooms or casinos. However, standards of cabin accommodation, food and service are commonly high.

Sea voyages last anything from three to twelve weeks. There is a heavy demand and you have to book from six to twelve months in advance. Weider Travel (see p 135) handle bookings for several cargo lines including Geest, who operate banana boats to and from the West Indies. Other sailings can be booked to destinations in Africa, Asia, Australasia, North and South America as well as in the Mediterranean.

Passengers must be prepared to be flexible; sailing schedules, ports of call and the duration of voyages can all be affected if the weather is bad or if the delivery of cargo to the port has been delayed. It should be noted that there is an age limit of 75 on some voyages since they can be 'eventful', and passengers over 65 must have a certificate from their GP stating that they are in good health.

CAMPING AND CARAVANNING

Camping or caravanning on the Continent often combines the joys of living in the great outdoors with the convenience of on-site toilets, showers and laundry facilities of a high standard. One great advantage of owning your own mobile accommodation is the opportunity it offers to pursue outdoor activities such as fishing, canoeing, horseriding or walking. Many continental sites, which have been located with these pursuits in mind, are reasonably uncrowded during May, June and September.

The main attractions of camping and caravanning for most people are the freedom of movement and the flexibility. This kind of holiday can work out a lot cheaper than one which incorporates hotel accommodation or conventional villa rental, so you may be able to afford to stay abroad for a longer period of time. However, economic reasons are not always a prime consideration, nor is this kind of holiday necessarily a cheap option. If you haven't been camping since your boy scout or girl guide days, then a visit to a camping and caravanning exhibition – like the yearly event at Olympia – to see the range of equipment now available can be quite an eye-opener.

A basic necessity is a car powerful enough to tow a caravan or trailer tent. An up-to-date alternative to the trailer tent is a folding camper, a sort of concertina caravan which is easy to erect and does not need pegging out. Motorised caravans are another good choice for older people because they do away with the whole business of towing, hitching and unhitching, which can all require a great deal of energy and stamina. Before embarking on this type of holiday, you should consider whether you would feel happy driving on roads abroad in a large vehicle, or towing an extra load.

It goes without saying that a long-stay camping or caravanning trip abroad is not a good idea for the uninitiated. If this sort of holiday appeals to you but you are an absolute beginner, then why not try out a short package holiday first with a company like Canvas Holidays or Eurocamp (see p 134). These organisations specialise in both long and short self-drive camping and mobile-home holidays at literally hundreds of quality sites in a wide range of countries, including France, Spain and Italy. Accommodation is in luxury tents or six to eight berth mobile homes, so sharing is a possibility. Both tents and mobile homes are fully equipped and have sprung beds, electric lighting and a kitchen with cooker and fridge. The mobile homes contain their own bathroom with shower, hot and cold water and flush toilet connected to main drainage. A bathroom is an additional extra to tents at some campsites; you need to check the brochure for details.

With these companies, you can travel on any day of the week and enjoy any length of stay. You choose the region from the brochure and the company books the site(s), along with the travel arrangements. There is a choice of ferry crossings or – if you don't want to drive all the way south – Motorail and flydrive options. May, June and September are quieter months and some companies offer holidaymakers three weeks' rental for the price of two at this time of year. Reservations staff are available to give advice and information, particularly for first-timers and people with a disability.

The ferry companies themselves are another good source for short package holidays, including chalet holiday sites, camping and caravanning. Their brochures are available from travel agents.

A final suggestion for first-time campers who want to try their hand is to contact an overseas campsite direct; perhaps one that has been warmly recommended by a like-minded friend. Many of these sites have caravans and mobile homes available for weekly hire and this is a convenient and independent way of having that first trial run.

If you have had a trial run which was a success and you are considering buying your own home-on-wheels, why not join the Camping and Caravanning Club – CCC (see p 134)? Its monthly magazine has helpful articles and news for regulars as well as beginners, and it also carries advertisements for new and used caravans and equipment.

Before actually parting with your money for a caravan, you may like to contact the RAC, which run a useful scheme called Carascan, an independent inspection service for used caravans. The peace of mind this buys is worth every penny of the small service fee.

You may well decide to hire both caravan and equipment to begin with, but when it comes to buying, it is false economy to skimp on equipment. The CCC advise you to buy the best you can afford – whether it is pots and pans or sleeping bags.

Membership of the CCC entitles you to several useful services. There is the Carefree Foreign Touring Service, which includes a Pitch Abroad Reservation Scheme, as well as an insurance package with Europ Assistance. The club can also supply you with an International Camping Carnet, an invaluable document which bears your photograph and saves having to hand over your passport at every European campsite. Club book sales include the annual *RAC/CCC Continental Camping and Caravanning Guide*, which lists sites in Western Europe.

A particular hazard of any outdoor-based holiday, especially camping and caravanning, is insect bites. These are not necessarily a health risk in themselves, but can be irritating and unpleasant enough to ruin this kind of holiday. Mosquito nets and insect repellants, tested by MASTA (the Medical Advisory Service for Travellers Abroad, based at the London School of Hygiene and Tropical Medicine) are available by mail order from the School or from British Airways Travel Clinics (see p 136).

VOLUNTARY WORK ABROAD

People who have travelled a great deal in their working lives, or have worked overseas, often find it more difficult than others to adjust to a life of leisure at home in the UK. But, of course, retirement should not be regarded as an inevitable limitation on an active life.

Volunteers with management, professional or technical skills are needed for short assignments of two to three months' duration by the British Executive Service Overseas – BESO (see p 136), which is an independent charity, funded by Government and donations from industry.

— *Doris Young*, who had run a family business for many years since the death of her father, spent seven weeks in Jamaica on a BESO assignment. As the managing director of her family's firm, which produces high-quality furniture, she had already travelled to many parts of the world buying timber. She also had experience in overseas marketing. BESO had received a request for help from a Jamaican company, employing about 220 people, that was on the verge of a new venture: the production of furniture and equipment for schools and Government departments. The company needed someone who could give them advice on the layout of workshops, machinery requirements and training.

Doris was received with enthusiasm. There were many areas where she was able to give help. For example, the company had virtually no control over materials, and it kept no proper records. She was able to suggest systems for control and organisation. There were logistical problems, too. For example, she noticed that the spraying department was situated right next door to the sand-papering department, and was able to suggest a more rational alternative. Occasionally, she couldn't help; there were some pieces of machinery she considered vital for certain areas of the company's operations, but they were unable to import them because of the insoluble problem of the country's shortage of foreign exchange.

Areas of industry where volunteers with up-to-date expertise are particularly needed include the following: textiles and clothing; food and drink processing; retailing; hotel management and tourism. BESO, which would particularly welcome more applications from women, pay the cost of air travel and insurance. Accommodation and subsistence are usually provided by the organisation requesting assistance.

More information on opportunities for volunteer work abroad is available from the Central Bureau for Educational Visits and Exchanges (see p 134). Full details of the requirements of over 100 organisations, many of which are religion-based, are listed in the publication *Volunteer Work*. Another potential source of help is a leaflet called *A Place for you Overseas – the Over-50s*, produced by the ecumenical organisation Christians Abroad (see p 134).

3

Long-Stay Holidays
Getting Ready To Go

Most people planning a two-week holiday abroad make lists. Much of this planning will still apply to a long-stay holiday but the main difference will be that the lists are going to be much lengthier. Many of the arrangements such as visa applications and immunisation jabs need to be seen to well in advance, by at least two to three months. Don't leave anything until the last minute.

Documentation

PASSPORTS

You should apply for or renew your passport well in advance of your journey, allowing for delays at the Passport Office. The new EC maroon-coloured passport is a national passport which has a common format with the passports of other member countries, and with its computer-readable magnetic strip, processing is much speedier.

The temporary British Vistors Passport, obtainable from the Post Office and valid for one year, is unsuitable for most long-stay holidays. Visa extensions and the remaining validity stamp required for certain countries (eg US, Yugoslavia) are only permissible on the full ten-year passports.

Passports with a previously stamped entry from one country are not always accepted in another country, if a politically sensitive situation exists between them (eg Israel and certain Arab countries). The Passport Office can issue a supplementary passport to cover these contingencies.

Whilst on holiday, it is strongly advisable to keep your passport on your person in a body belt or to lock it away in a safe place. In the event of loss or theft, you should notify the local police immediately and take their report to the nearest British Consular offices. Before leaving the UK, it would be worth photocopying the first four pages of your passport to take with you, as this information could help speed up the issue of a replacement by the British Consulate abroad.

VISAS

Visas may be required for stays of more than a certain duration; eg 60 days in Portugal, 90 days in Spain. Rules vary according to country and are subject to alteration. You should personally check you have the latest information for your destination. Do *not* rely solely on advice from your travel agent or tour operator's brochure. The responsibility for valid passports and visas is yours. You should allow plenty of time for your visa application to be processed.

Information concerning residency rules can be obtained from the appropriate foreign consulate or national tourist office here in the UK, and it is essential to do this research before leaving the country. A visa extension can, however, be obtained abroad if you travel to the appropriate office, wherever this may be.

Financial arrangements

DAY-TO-DAY FINANCE

Your financial requirements for a long-stay holiday will be rather different from the arrangements you usually make for a short holiday. Also, the kind of holiday and the location will both affect the decision on how to take your money. It is preferable to rely on a variety of sources for funds, bearing in mind that some options may not be effective in rural areas.

The most common sources of funds open to you are:

- UK bank notes
- Foreign currency in cash
- Cash cards
- Traveller's cheques
- Eurocheques
- Credit cards

Each source has *advantages* and *disadvantages*.

UK bank notes

♦ These can be exchanged for local currency at any bank; rates may be more favourable than buying foreign currency in the UK.

♦ The exchange rate is less favourable than for traveller's cheques.

♦ With the £5-note you are able to exchange a smaller denomination than with traveller's cheques.

♦ If you lose them, they have gone.

Foreign currency in cash

♦ It is vital to have low-denomination cash on arrival to meet minor expenses such as road tolls, on-the-spot motoring fines, taxis, drinks, phone calls, tips, etc.

♦ It is useful at weekends and on public holidays when banks are closed.

♦ It is necessary for incidental purchases: petrol, food, etc.

♦ In large quantities you risk loss or theft.

Cash cards

♦ Such cards' usefulness depends greatly on your destination. There are growing numbers of automatic cash dispensers in major towns, but very few in rural areas. Obtain a list of their locations from your bank before your departure.

Traveller's cheques

♦ Safety is the major advantage. You have to sign them twice in the presence of a bank cashier; when you buy them and when you cash them. If they are lost or stolen, you will be reimbursed.

♦ The minimum denomination is £10.

Eurocheques

♦ These are a useful method of drawing on your UK bank account as and when you need to. The bulk of your holiday money stays in your bank account until you need it, whereas with traveller's cheques, for example, you have to withdraw the money before your departure.

♦ They are useful if you are going to more than one country and more than one currency is involved.

♦ You can write out a cheque not only in any currency, but also for an exact amount, to settle a bill in a restaurant, for example.

♦ You can only obtain further cheques and/or a cheque guarantee card in the country of origin, so ensure you have enough cheques (there are only 20 per book) and that your card is not nearing its expiry date.

♦ They are difficult to recoup if lost or stolen. Always keep the card separate from the Eurocheque book for security.

♦ There is a minimum handling charge which makes them uneconomic for small amounts.

Credit cards

♦ No prior arrangements are necessary. You can just 'up and go'.

♦ They are particularly recommended for car hire and can obviate the need to pay a deposit.

♦ They are useful in an emergency as a fallback.

♦ They are not widely accepted away from tourist areas or in petrol stations.

♦ They are difficult to replace abroad in the event of loss or theft.

♦ The rate of exchange is established by the date that the credit-card company receives their copy of the voucher.

Consequently, you won't know exactly how much has been charged to your account (in sterling).

♦ Accumulated payments will incur interest charges unless you have arranged for your bank to make a monthly payment to the credit-card company.

STATE PENSIONS

Going abroad on a long-stay holiday does not affect entitlement to a retirement or widows' pension. However, you will have to decide how you would like it to be paid while you are away. Whatever you decide, make sure you inform the Department of Social Security (DSS) of any absence over three months.

The most straightforward arrangement, and one that ensures easy access to your money abroad, is to have your pension paid direct into a bank or building society account. Many people do this already. Complete Form NI 105, which is obtainable from your local DSS office, and allow at least four weeks for the new arrangement to take effect.

For a stay lasting longer than three months, the local DSS office can make arrangements to send your pension abroad for you to cash locally. However, payment will be made in arrears and at intervals of four to thirteen weeks. Apply to the DSS at least one month in advance of your departure.

If your overseas stay is to be for less than three months, you can let your weekly orders accumulate and cash them as a lump sum at the post office as usual on your return. They must be cashed within three months of the date stamped on them; if you leave them longer, you will have to return the order book to the DSS for a refund.

It is possible, if difficult, to nominate a trusted person to receive your pension for you while you are away. This could be useful if you want any bills paid in your absence. This method of payment is in arrears and at four to thirteen week intervals. Apply to your local DSS office for information.

OTHER BENEFITS

Any extended stay abroad, even a visit to your family on an air ticket which they have paid for, is a change of circumstances which may well affect any other State benefits you hold.

Before considering individual benefits in turn, here are a few general points.

♦ Some benefits are not payable while you are abroad, and you should inform the appropriate authority (eg the DSS or the local authority of your trip, in order to qualify for the resumption of payment on your return. *Request individual advice.* Tell them if a family visit is involved and any other special circumstances. Keep a copy of all correspondence between you and the relevant office.

♦ The complex rules covering the payment of State benefits are further complicated by the regulations within your country of destination, and still further by whether it is an EC country or one with a reciprocal arrangement with the UK. Leaflet NI 38 *Social Security Abroad*, obtainable from the DSS Overseas Branch (see p 137), contains a list of countries with whom the UK has a reciprocal agreement, and each has its own advisory leaflet.

More detailed information is contained in *The Disability Rights Handbook*, published each year in April by the Disability Alliance ERA (see p 142). There may be a copy in your local library, but make sure it is the most up-to-date edition.

The following summary of benefits gives *general guidelines only.* You should seek advice to cover your individual circumstances.

Income support

This is allowable to pensioners for the first four weeks only of a temporary absence abroad. It is paid retrospectively on your return.

Housing benefit and community charge benefit

Housing benefit for rent and rate rebates is available to cover absences from home of up to one year, but not if you sublet your house while you are away. The community charge (or poll tax) replaced rates in Scotland in April 1989 and will be introduced in England and Wales from April 1990. You will have to pay the personal community charge if the local authority decides your 'sole or main residence' is in the area. If you are liable for the charge you can claim a rebate even if you are temporarily away from home.

Invalidity benefit and severe disablement allowance

These depend on circumstances. If you have been continuously incapable of work for at least six months previously, a short holiday abroad should pose no problem. An extended stay may need further explanation. Payments of these benefits abroad is at the discretion of the Secretary of State, although the decision is taken locally at the DSS office. Make sure that any special circumstances involved are understood, such as a visit to family abroad. There is no right of appeal, but a letter from a doctor, social worker or MP might get a decision reversed.

Health care

CHECK-UPS

You wouldn't dream of taking your car on a long-distance journey, without giving it a good mechanical overhaul first. Your body needs an overhaul too, especially if you intend being abroad for a lengthy stay. A lot of anxiety, inconvenience and illness can be prevented by taking a few simple precautions. Before you go, make an appointment with the following professionals, informing them of your forthcoming trip.

A doctor
A dentist
A chiropodist
An ophthalmic optician

A doctor

Your GP will give you a check-up before your departure. An appointment is especially important if you are on continuous medication, such as tablets for high blood pressure, and need sufficient supplies to cover your entire stay. An explanatory note from your GP is a safeguard in case customs officials query large quantities of tablets. It is also vital for your GP to write down the dosage of any drug you require, and its generic as well as brand name, in the event of your having to obtain emergency supplies from a doctor overseas.

A dentist

Your dentist will check for worn dentures, fillings and crowns, all of which could avoid expensive treatment abroad. Medical insurance covers emergency treatment only, not this kind of restoration work. Another point to remember is that saving a tooth is not always a priority abroad; extraction is much more common. Another good reason to see your dentist before you go.

A chiropodist

Your chiropodist will ensure your feet are in good shape for all the additional, and possibly unaccustomed, walking involved in sightseeing and exploring.

An ophthalmic optician

It would be advisable to buy a spare pair of glasses to take with you as a standby. It is also worth obtaining a note of your current lens prescription from an optician in case of accidents. A good pair of prescription sunglasses could be a worthwhile investment; you should be wearing them more often than you do at home. People who use contact lenses are recommended to take a spare pair of glasses in case of eye irritation in a warmer, dryer climate. Obviously, you should also pack generous supplies of your usual cleansing and soaking solutions.

IMMUNISATION

Obtaining information about the appropriate jabs necessary for anywhere even slightly off the beaten track used to be a difficult, time-consuming process, involving phone calls to embassies, appointments with GPs (who did not necessarily know the most up-to-date requirements of individual countries) and trips to remote yellow-fever clinics held on just one afternoon a week. All this has changed.

You can still go to your GP of course. Phone the surgery and ask the receptionist how immunisations are handled at that practice. There will probably be a regular time when these things are dealt with, outside normal surgery hours. Bear in mind that your GP is entitled to charge you for these services.

British Airways Travel Clinics (see p 136) are an alternative source of advice and treatment. These are a joint venture with MASTA. One of their facilities is a database containing regularly updated information on health problems in 230 countries. This is obviously very useful for travellers. Holidaymakers (travelling with *any* airline, incidentally) can pay for individual advice, and any necessary immunisations and vaccinations. Such advice may well be important since older people are a special group; they may never have been offered polio vaccine, for example, which is advisable for anyone travelling outside Northern Europe or Northern America. As well as immunisations, vaccinations and authoritative advice, these clinics also sell recommended and tested items such as water filters, insect repellents and mosquito nets.

MASTA offer their own information service in the form of individual health briefs, based on your medical history, and you can obtain application forms for these from Boots pharmacies. Alternatively, you can write to MASTA directly (see p 138).

HOLIDAY HEALTH HAZARDS

The main holiday hazards for visitors to warm climates still apply on long-stay holidays. You should take care with the following.

Sunburn

Diarrhoea

Insect bites

Prevention is better than the cure in every case. Why suffer the discomfort for the sake of a few simple measures?

Sunburn

♦ Treat the sun with respect, as the locals do. Do not overdo the exposure, particularly for the first few days. Twenty minutes' sunbathing is ample on the first occasion, using a sun cream or oil containing a high sun protection factor (SPF). As your skin gets acclimatised, change to a cream or oil with a lower SPF.

♦ A wide-brimmed hat keeps your head cool. It also keeps the sun off your face and out of your eyes.

♦ A mild tan looks healthy and flattering, but a tanned leathery skin is ageing. Both men and women should use plenty of moisturising cream to counteract the drying effects of the sun and wind.

♦ You can get sunburnt without meaning to, by falling asleep in a chair on a balcony or beside a pool; it is easily done. Be alert for your companion as well.

♦ Sunburn is painful and irritating. Calamine lotion is still the most soothing remedy for mild sunburn, but severe sunburn should be treated as for a heat burn. Protect the area and keep it clean. Remember to take extra care to stay out of the sun for the next few days.

Diarrhoea

♦ Most holiday diarrhoea is caused by food or drink. In most cases, recovery will take from 48-72 hours, and you must ensure an adequate intake of non-alcoholic drinks to prevent dehydration.

♦ Avoid eating anything with a high risk of contamination, eg shellfish from the heavily polluted Mediterranean and Adriatic coasts, which carry more risk than shellfish from the Atlantic coast.

♦ Water contamination, a frequent cause of the complaint, is passed not only through drinking water, but also by way of (washed) salads, ice cubes and ice cream. Standards of water purity are, in fact, higher in most EC countries than they are in the UK.

♦ Be scrupulous about washing and drying your hands, and peel all fruit before eating it.

Insect bites

♦ Popular breeding grounds for mosquito-like insects are near water and in shady woods – the very spots often chosen for camping and caravanning sites. Preventive measures like insect repellents and mosquito nets are absolute 'musts' for this type of holiday (see p 58).

♦ First-aid kits should contain a soothing antiseptic cream to relieve the itch and prevent scratching.

EMERGENCY TREATMENT ABROAD

No one likes to think of having emergency medical treatment while they are abroad but, again, it is better to be safe than sorry. Making adequate preparations before you leave will avoid a great deal of anxiety and inconvenience at a time when you are already vulnerable.

For free emergency treatment in EC countries, you need an important document called E111, obtainable from the DSS. An application form for E111 is contained in the useful DSS booklet SA 40

Before You Go (available at your local office or to order on the Freephone service 0800-555777). The facts about E111 are set out below.

- It will be valid for all future temporary visits abroad, for as long as you are normally resident in the UK.

- It proves your entitlement to State health care in any EC country, but only on the same basis as nationals (which is seldom as comprehensive and straightforward as it is in the UK). You may be charged for some elements of your treatment, eg hospital accommodation and/or drugs, and you will have to apply for refunds on these charges when you return to the UK.

- It covers emergency treatment only. Dental treatment may be borderline; an abscess or infection may be interpreted as an emergency, a lost filling may not.

- It does not cover the cost of repatriation in the event of serious illness or death. The DSS recommends private medical cover for anyone holidaying abroad. If you belong to a private medical insurance scheme, check if you are covered abroad.

The DSS booklet SA 41 *While You're Away* contains additional, detailed information about E111, including how to claim refunds for emergency treatment you have received.

Free emergency medical treatment is also available in certain countries which have a reciprocal agreement with the UK, including Australia, New Zealand, Malta and Yugoslavia. You will need documentary evidence to prove your entitlement to treatment: a UK passport, proof of UK residence and, in some cases, an NHS medical card. Full details of the relevant countries and their individual requirements can be found in the DSS booklet SA 40 *Before You Go*.

Travel insurance

Unlike the various insurance policies you take out and renew each year – life insurance, home contents insurance, property insurance and so on – travel insurance is generally sold as a 'package', which includes all the different kinds of cover you need while you are abroad, other than car insurance. The right insurance package will not only give you full medical cover, but will also cover your money and belongings, the cancellation or curtailment of your holiday, delayed baggage, delayed departure and personal liability. You can 'shop around' for insurance, just as you do for holidays. Do not feel that you have to accept the tour operator's insurance package; you may be able to find an alternative which is more appropriate for you and your circumstances.

MEDICAL COVER

You need sufficient private medical cover to pay for comprehensive treatment in the event of illness or accident, and also in case you need to be flown home by air ambulance. This latter eventuality is not covered by the emergency treatment available under E111 or by the reciprocal health care arrangements with certain other countries (see p 61).

Some policies charge higher premiums for medical cover if you are over 65. This may be unavoidable. What you are looking for, as an older holidaymaker, is value for money and adequate cover – not cut-price insurance.

The cover being offered as part of a package-holiday insurance scheme may well be suitable for your needs. Details given in the brochures, however, are only an abbreviated version. Ask to see the full policy. Older travellers need to check for exclusion clauses, particularly those relating to previous illness.

Travel agents may also provide their own travel insurance packages. Sometimes they even offer a discount or reduction on the price of their holidays if you agree to buy this insurance. Again, ask to see the full details of the policy and look carefully at restrictive or exclusion clauses.

Many policies exclude cover for recent illness or a pre-existing medical condition, such as heart trouble, unless this is disclosed at the time and accepted by the insurers. You should always disclose a pre-existing medical condition, even if the policy does not ask you to. You may have to pay a higher premium but this is preferable to a disputed claim later in the day.

Of course, you may already have private medical insurance with a company that has a comprehensive holiday insurance available as an 'add-on'. Alternatively, for a long stay of a few months, your existing health-care insurers may grant a reduced premium on your existing cover if you decide to take up the tour operator's insurance package. Saga, for example, include all travel insurance and medical cover in the cost of their holidays; there is no point in paying twice.

CANCELLATION AND CURTAILMENT

It is vital that the possible cancellation or curtailment of your holiday is covered, in order that expensive tickets and/or deposits are not lost. Again, read the full policy on offer with care. Exclusion clauses can also apply here and you will need to think specifically about your particular circumstances. For example, you may have to cancel your holiday in order to look after a sick relative. Some policies will not cover this. You may have been planning to spend a holiday with family or friends. If your host is ill, you may have to cancel. Not all policies will pay compensation.

PERSONAL BELONGINGS

On a long-stay holiday you may well be taking expensive items which are not normally part of your holiday luggage – a radio-cassette player, perhaps – in addition to the more usual cameras and video equipment. You need to ensure that these items are adequately covered in the event of loss or damage. Your existing home contents policy may well contain a worldwide 'all-risks' clause but, even if it does, check that the value of goods covered in this way is not unduly limited. You can get advice on extra cover from an insurance broker.

FURTHER ADVICE

The other components of travel insurance, such as delayed baggage, departure and personal liability will all be explained in the full policy that you are considering. Query any unduly restrictive clauses.

The consumer magazine *Holiday Which?* carries regularly updated information on the best buys in travel insurance, and also quotes examples of bad practice. A leaflet from the Office of Fair Trading (see p 143) also provides further background information.

If long-stay holidays are going to be part of your future way of life, the one-off holiday insurance package might not be such a good idea. Frequent travellers often adopt annual schemes including worldwide year-round travel cover. You can always consult an insurance broker for a package tailored to your needs. The British Insurance Investment Brokers Association (BIIBA) will supply addresses of local members (see p 136).

CONSUMER PROTECTION

Consumer protection is another form of guarantee for your flight or holiday, in the event of your travel company going bankrupt. These guarantees, one provided by ABTA, a travel association, the other by means of a special licence, an ATOL, were introduced in order to reassure the holiday-buying public that they could buy with confidence.

ABTA, which stands for the Association of British Travel Agents (see p 136), operates codes of conduct which have been drawn up in conjunction with the Office of Fair Trading. There is also an agreement to deal with complaints quickly and fairly. In addition, there are procedures in the case of a company's financial failure, eg the provision of a speedy refund or an offer of another holiday of the same standard.

As the consumer, you need to make sure that the tour operator whose holiday you wish to buy is an ABTA member. If you make your booking through a travel agent, then the agent must also be a member. If your tour operator then goes out of business, your holiday is protected. Always look for the ABTA symbol.

The Association offers a free conciliation service for complaints about its members, but only after you have already tried to reach a settlement yourself. If the conciliation service fails to resolve your disagreement, you can choose to use the independent low-cost, documents-only arbitration scheme set up by the Institute of Arbitrators especially for clients of ABTA members. This should be approached with care. While the conciliation service does not remove your right to seek legal action, the arbitration scheme operates as an *alternative* to going to court. Many aggrieved holidaymakers have found the Small Claims Court procedures (for claims of £500 or below) both simple and successful. Neither the conciliation service nor the arbitration scheme is available for claims involving physical injury or illness.

ATOL stands for the Air Travel Organiser's Licence. The licence is granted by the Civil Aviation Authority and is a legal requirement for anyone selling charter air holidays or charter seats to the public. (Scheduled flights bought direct from an airline or a travel agent are not covered by this system.) The consumer is protected through a fully backed-up bond guarantee. Every ATOL holder has a registered number which appears on their logo.

In connection with this, a free leaflet *Protecting Your Air Holiday* is available from the Civil Aviation Authority (see p 136).

You and your car

TAKING YOUR CAR ABROAD

Taking your car abroad gives you freedom and flexibility and, therefore, a greater range of holidays to choose from. Many villa rentals, for example, would be out of the question without your own transport. Another not insignificant advantage is that you can take a great deal more baggage with you in a car than you can on a plane, which may be important to you on a long-stay holiday.

You may never have taken your car abroad before, or if you have done so, it may have been a long time ago. Motoring abroad in spring and autumn can be a quite different and enjoyable experience, described by one retired holidaymaker as 'just how it used to be in the old days'. Sometimes there is hardly another car on the road, particularly if you choose scenic routes and avoid toll roads.

A good introduction to driving abroad before taking your own vehicle is to experiment with a few days' continental car hire while you are on a regular holiday (a few tips about foreign car hire are included on p 67). This will give you the experience of driving on the right (if appropriate!) and the opportunity to familiarise yourself with road signs.

If you do decide to take your own car, you will find that the main difficulty in using a car with right-hand drive on the Continent is overtaking. With the traffic in front obscuring your view, you have to either rely on the person in the passenger seat, or, if you're alone, pull out cautiously into the path of oncoming traffic. A helpful device is a Euromirror, which you attach to the passenger side of the windscreen where it enables you to see forward on the lefthand side.

Before leaving for your holiday, you will need to acquaint yourself not only with the general rules for driving in Europe, but also with specific regulations for the countries you intend driving in. An RAC/AA approved GB plate is compulsory, as is a red warning triangle in the event of breakdown or accident. On-the-spot fines are common in many countries for failing to comply with these regulations and for other transgressions such as non-dipped headlights.

When driving abroad you need to carry the following documents with you:

A full UK driving licence
A green card
A bail bond (Spain only)

UK driving licence

♦ This must be a full licence and must be current.

♦ The old green licence is not always recognised and for some countries, such as Spain, Italy and Greece, you also need an International Driving Permit (IDP), obtainable from the AA or RAC. Holders of the more recently issued pink EC licences do not require this, but since local difficulties may arise over its acceptance, an IDP is recommended.

Green card

♦ This is obtainable from your insurers, and is the only readily acceptable international evidence that the driver has insurance above the minimum. It is a proof that you are insured against all damage you may cause to others if you are involved in a motor accident.

Bail bond

♦ This is recommended for driving in Spain, where accidents may have serious consequences; a car may be impounded, the driver may be kept in custody. The bond can be obtained from your insurers, the AA or the RAC.

Detailed, up-to-date advice on all aspects of motoring abroad is available from the AA and RAC. Local branches have a range of leaflets explaining their many services for travellers abroad.

CAR HIRE ABROAD

An alternative to taking your car abroad is hiring a vehicle on your arrival. Many people find this an attractive option but considerable care should be taken before any agreement is signed.

One of the most important aspects of car rental is making sure you have adequate insurance cover. If you don't have Collision Damage

Waiver (CDW), you will be liable for the first £250 or more of accidental damage to the hired vehicle, irrespective of whose fault it was.

In the US, the minimum level of third party insurance is fixed by individual states, which is why you must always inform the car rental company if you intend driving out of state. By UK standards, US third party cover is low, so most British tour companies will offer 'top-up' insurance on any flydrive package.

Free car hire, frequently offered on Florida holidays, is not always the attractive perk it might seem. You may be required to pay the full cost of insurance which can work out to be more expensive than an inclusive local self-drive rate.

LEAVING YOUR CAR AT HOME

If you are going abroad for a lengthy stay of a month or more, and leaving your car at home, it may be worth your while to apply for a refund or negotiate a reduction on two expensive items:

The road fund licence
Car insurance

Road fund licence

- Rebates are obtainable for *complete calendar months only*, if your car is off the public highway. Form V14, obtainable from a post office, must be completed and posted to the DVLC, Swansea SA99 1AL in good time before the first day of the month for which you are claiming.

- Claiming a rebate cancels your road fund licence. You will have to re-tax your car before you can use it on your return. Whether the amount of rebate is worth the trouble will depend on how many months you are away.

- To obtain a new road fund licence you will need an insurance certificate, or temporary cover note, and (if required) a current MOT test certificate. Your MOT test can be done in advance, before you go.

Car insurance

- ♦ Reductions are allowable for a period over 28 days. They are usually referred to as 'laid-up rebates' and the terms vary from company to company. Some will insist that the car is kept in a locked garage, a wise precaution if the car is to be unused while you are away.

Domestic arrangements

Leaving the country for any period of time obviously necessitates a number of domestic arrangements. The following will all require some special thought and preparation.

Home security
The central heating system
Electrical appliances
The water supply
Outstanding and recurring bills
Deliveries and subscriptions

Home security

Most housebreaking is opportunistic, so your aim should be to 'remove' as many of the opportunities as you possibly can. Ideally, you want your house to give the appearance of being occupied and this is obviously going to be a problem if you are away for months at a time. The well-known give-away clues that indicate an absent owner are:

free newspapers and junk mail stuck in a letterbox or lying in the porch;
uncut grass;
empty, unused dustbins.

There is no substitute for a small team of relatives, friends and/or neighbours who, between them, will keep an eye on the place for you.

As well as dealing with eyesores, they can help create the impression of the house being lived in by perhaps:

switching on lights in the evening;

drawing curtains, closing and opening blinds;

leaving a radio or TV on in the evening;

parking their car in your drive.

You might consider paying a nominal caretaking allowance to someone you know to be trustworthy and reliable, particularly for a month's absence or more. If you belong to a Neighbourhood Watch scheme, the local co-ordinator may be able to suggest a possible 'minder' from among other members.

A few specific security tips worth considering are given below.

♦ Jewellery and other valuables should be stored elsewhere, perhaps with a friend, relative or neighbour, as should your video or hi-fi equipment.

♦ Advice on burglar-proofing your home can be obtained free of charge from the Crime Prevention Officer at your local police station.

♦ Consider fitting a burglar alarm. By law, the local police should have the names, addresses and phone numbers of two keyholders for any property fitted with an alarm. Both the police and environmental health officers have the right to enter a property in order to stop an alarm which has been set off accidentally. During an extended stay abroad, it would be useful to supply details of a third keyholder.

♦ Inform the insurance company that covers your property and home contents of any proposed lengthy absence. In order for your cover to be maintained, they may insist on some extra security precautions. For example, they invariably insist on mortice locks being fitted to front and back doors, as well as screw-type locks being fixed on all windows.

♦ Outbuildings, such as garden sheds, garages and greenhouses, are never totally secure. Tools and other valuable equipment should be stored elsewhere while you are away.

The central heating system

Consult your insurance company on this matter. Some older policies require radiator systems to be drained if the property is to be unoccupied for any length of time. In this case, you may need the assistance of a plumber or heating engineer.

Many of the modern systems cannot be completely drained. Sometimes, where the system includes a corrosion inhibitor such as 'Fernox', instructions will specifically state: 'Do not drain'. As an alternative to draining, you could ask the insurance company if they will accept the use of a special antifreeze product (*not* car antifreeze), which will protect the system down to a temperature of $-15°C$ ($2°F$). A safe choice, and the most widely available product for domestic use is 'Alphi-11', manufactured by Fernox, which lasts for at least six years. Remember, you can only use an antifreeze product in a system which has a separate header tank. The tank should be well insulated, as should the pipes up from the heating system.

Some form of minimal heating during the time a property is unoccupied reduces the risk of severe condensation particularly in older buildings. A frost-protection thermostat fitted to your radiator or warm-air system will automatically switch on the heating if the inside temperature drops below $5°C$ ($40°F$). Alternatively, you can arrange for minimal heating to come on for a short period each day.

If you have gas central heating, you should arrange to have the boiler serviced before you go away. Your heating engineer will check that the thermocouple is working properly. This is an important device which turns off the gas in the event of the pilot flame failing.

Electrical appliances

There are a number of straightforward precautions which are worth taking to ensure your electrical appliances are safe while you are away.

- ♦ Turn off the main cooker switch.
- ♦ Empty, wash and dry the fridge. Avoid leaving the door wide open

– a clear indication to a burglar of an unoccupied home. Instead, stick a wedge of paper to the fridge, in a position that will prevent the door from closing. The door then looks closed to anyone who is looking in, but the fridge will have sufficient airflow to prevent mould from growing.

♦ Empty, wash and dry the freezer, wedging the door open as for the fridge. (Check your insurance policy if you are leaving the freezer full.)

♦ Unplug all electrical appliances throughout the house.

♦ Disconnect all external radio or TV aerials from their receivers, in case of lightning.

The water supply

Your water supply should also be attended to; the following precautions are recommended.

♦ Turn off the water at the mains.

♦ Drain down most of the main cold water tank (leaving a level of about five centimetres/two inches above the highest outlet pipe).

♦ Flush the toilet and, if there is no separate shut-off valve, tie up the ballcock. This will prevent an overflow if left for a long time.

Outstanding and recurring bills

You will need to foresee and arrange payment of bills likely to arrive in your absence, notably for the gas, electricity, water and rates, as well as those from credit-card companies. The following options are worth considering.

♦ Set up a monthly direct debit or standing order from your bank or building society account, so long as you remember to allow at least a month for this to take effect.

♦ Inform all the relevant accounts offices of your dates of absence. Do this in writing and keep a copy of your letter. Offer them an advance payment, otherwise you may return to the UK to find yourself not only 'cut off' but also liable for hefty reconnection charges.

♦ Send credit-card companies an advance payment, sufficient to cover recent expenditure; otherwise you will incur interest charges.

♦ If your credit card is directly linked to your bank, make prior arrangements to pay your credit-card account out of funds from your current account.

Deliveries and subscriptions

Don't forget to attend to the following matters before you depart:
cancel the milk;
cancel your newspapers;
tell the window cleaner;
deal with any outstanding mail-order business;
review your subscriptions.

FORWARDING ADDRESS

An absolute must is to leave with a neighbour, or in a prominent place, a forwarding address and a telephone number where you can be contacted in an emergency.

Your personal packing

Packing for a long-stay holiday abroad, particularly in the low season, demands a certain degree of care and forethought. During a two- to three-week summer break in the southern Mediterranean you can more or less guarantee hot, sunny days and balmy evenings. A stay of a month or more in spring or autumn is a quite different proposition. You will meet with a much greater range of weather and temperatures, all depending of course on your country of destination, the season, the altitude and the proximity of the coast (see p 26). Do remember to pack an umbrella and some wet-weather gear, in addition to a warm jumper or cardigan. You may not have experienced heavy rain on the Continent before, but it's just as wet as ours!

A number of useful items for long-stay holidays are the following:

a strong torch;

a set of rechargeable batteries, for your radio and torch, together with a battery charger;

a Continental plug adaptor;

knitting, sewing or craftwork;

games: playing cards, etc;

a corkscrew: neither the lever kind nor the reverse thread type is widely available outside the UK and France;

a hot-water bottle;

tea bags;

plenty of reading material, crosswords, etc.

One obvious advantage of travelling by car is that you can take a great deal more with you. If you are flying, bear in mind that the baggage weight restriction for European air travel is only 20 kilos (44 lbs), however long your stay!

Special requirements

ON YOUR OWN?

Do you enjoy travel, but can't face holidaying alone? It's not surprising if you can't; most people tend to share this reluctance. Travelling on your own can be a depressing and lonely experience and there are practical drawbacks, too, like having to pay high supplements for a single room (usually in the worst part of the hotel) and, often, poor service from waiters in restaurants and hotel dining rooms.

A number of agencies and clubs now specialise in putting solo would-be travellers in touch with each other.

Solitaire (see p 138) is a nationwide self-help organisation, run by women for other women who are lonely in retirement. One of their services is a holiday register in which members can make contact with others who are interested in sharing a holiday.

Saga (see p 135) has a club magazine containing a 'Penfriends and Partnerships' section, where male and female members can advertise for travel companions. Only a small number of ads are actually printed in the magazine but full listings are sent to all interested members.

Travel Companions (see p 135) is a nationwide introduction agency for people of both sexes aged 30-75. It is *not* a dating agency, and most of the clients are women, seeking fellow women travellers.

Vera Coppard and Lisa Harrison, the women behind Travel Companions, are both travel-loving widows, who were themselves introduced to each other as a possible solution to holidaying alone. Before meeting Vera, Lisa had already tried a coach tour – a frequent recommendation for women on their own – only to find that the party consisted of 23 couples and herself!

Vera cites many practical, reciprocal advantages – particularly for an older woman – to travelling with a companion.

♦ There is someone to look after the luggage while you go to the toilet, make a phone call, or enquire about timetables, delayed departures, etc.

♦ A fellow explorer is prudent in countries which are not recommended for a woman on her own.

♦ There is someone to share costs, ie car hire, boat hire, etc.

♦ There is safety in numbers, not only in city streets after dark, but also in social situations. Many couples find it difficult to relate to a single person, even one who mixes easily with strangers. Having a companion makes it easier for a woman to hold her own in mixed company, and to buy a drink for a stranger without it being misconstrued.

♦ It is not only single people who may value a travel companion. A married person may well appreciate the company of a fellow traveller who perhaps shares an interest in, for example, art or walking, unlike their partner.

Vera and Lisa provide guidelines to prospective clients. They make the interesting observation that friends are often the last people you should share a holiday with; strangers put in more effort to make a holiday a success. Even a close, longlasting friendship does not automatically mean compatability on holiday, where day-to-day likes and dislikes and shared interests are more important than intimacy. Habits like smoking or reading into the night can spell disaster to the success of a holiday and, sadly, can result in the end of the friendship.

Prospective clients of Travel Companions complete an extensive questionnaire which covers personality traits, knowledge of languages and hobbies, as well as habits such as smoking. A professional approach to matching, plus a willingness on the part of clients to be flexible has resulted in some mutually highly satisfactory arrangements.

— **Marion and Joan**, two retired women, met through Travel Companions and rented an apartment together for a month in the south of France. On their original application form, they had each made quite different suggestions regarding which country they wanted to visit! Both, however, wanted to get away for a month during the winter. What they had in common was a love of art. Their professional backgrounds were similar, too, both having worked in personnel management. They were also matched because they lived within a convenient travelling distance of each other, which made the preliminary meetings between them all the easier.

Marion and Joan first spoke on the telephone and arranged to meet in London at Waterloo Station. One of them later confessed to an attack of last-minute nerves on her way to the meeting: 'What am I doing – going to meet a total stranger in this way?' After a meal in a nearby restaurant, their doubts eased away.

After this first meeting, they shared a weekend hotel break, which was on neutral ground. This was followed by further weekends in each other's homes, a good idea considering they intended sharing an apartment and would be thrown together much more than in a hotel. During these weekends, they ironed out lots of minor details, such as preferences for going to bed early or late. The outcome, the result of preparation and a degree of compromise, was a successful winter holiday, shared by two like-minded people, and with the added bonus of more travel in the future.

DISABILITIES

Don't ever be premature in deciding that your days of holidaying in the sun are over. It may be harder to get about, doing the shopping and getting on and off buses as you get older. You may get easily tired after an operation or serious illness, but so long as your GP does not think a holiday would be unwise, then it is a matter of assessing your limitations and finding ways round them. A long-stay holiday will need more careful planning than a shorter break, and you will have to anticipate possible problems; for example, if you wear a hearing aid, you will need to take a supply of the appropriate batteries. Not only might the right kind be difficult to find abroad; they will probably be much more expensive.

Opportunities for people with disabilities to go abroad are improving, and an increasing number of tour operators, travel agents and providers of transport and accommodation are paying attention to people with special needs. You will have to research and plan your long-stay holiday more carefully than other travellers, but the following specialist advice is available.

♦ RADAR (see p 138) publishes an annually updated guide for disabled people called *Holidays and Travel Abroad*. This covers transport services and accommodation in various countries, as well as listing helpful organisations.

♦ Holiday Care Service (see p 137) is a charity providing free information and advice on all aspects of travel in response to individual enquiries from elderly and disabled people. The Holiday Care Service also runs a special scheme called 'Holiday Helpers', which finds experienced volunteers as holiday carers/companions for anyone who seeks that extra support on holiday.

♦ London Regional Transport (LRT) Unit for Disabled Passengers (see p 138) can advise travellers passing through the capital en route for the Continent. LRT runs the Carelink service, which provides specially designed buses, with lifts for wheelchairs. The buses connect with London's mainline railway stations and with wheelchair-accessible Airbus services (at Euston and Victoria) which run to and from Heathrow.

♦ The British Diabetic Association (see p 136) can advise diabetic travellers on a range of matters, from monitoring blood sugar levels to the best buys in travel insurance. One chapter in a travel book compiled by Dr Richard Dawood, *How to Stay Healthy Abroad* (see p 142), is devoted to diabetic travellers and gives information on how injection routines are affected by time changes during long-distance air travel. The major hazard is hypoglycaemia, so diabetics should always carry sugar on them and make sure that their companion knows how to help if this occurs.

Some form of identification is recommended. It may prove useful for passing through Customs with a supply of hypodermic syringes, but – more importantly – it may prove vital in the event of a collapse. Many diabetics wear the identity bracelet from Medic-Alert (see p 138), which is also useful for other travellers with a known allergy, rare blood groups, or other non-obvious medical conditions.

OLDER TRAVELLERS

British Airways offers the following advice to older passengers. Much of it applies to all travellers – young and old. Other airlines offer similar advice and services.

♦ Please tell whoever makes your booking if you are on a special diet. We have a range of special meals available on most flights. Just give us 24 hours to provide them.

♦ If you need a special seat, for example, in the smoking area or near the toilet, do tell whoever makes your reservation or the person who checks you in for your flight at the airport.

♦ Airports often involve walking fairly long distances. If you find this difficult please let us know so that we can arrange a wheelchair or buggy to transport you to and from the aircraft.

♦ If you need our help to reach your seat on the aircraft, please let us know so that we can take you on board before other passengers.

Second thoughts

With your impending departure only a matter of days away, you may well be asking yourself whose idea this holiday was in the first place? Will it be worth all the trouble. What if the trip turns out to be a disappointment, and a waste of time and money?

Calm down. Life is full of 'what if?'s. Your priority is to sort out the genuine areas of concern (anxiety about an older relative, perhaps, who is not in the best of health) from the last-minute attack of nerves. Nerves are a perfectly natural reaction. Going abroad for a month or more is for many people a huge adventure – especially the first time. Provided that you have made careful back-up arrangements and not left things to chance, what are you worrying about? There are usually well-proven procedures for dealing with most of life's emergencies. Here are a couple of extreme examples.

WHAT IF SOME LOCAL POLITICAL ACTIVITY FLARES UP IN MY COUNTRY OF DESTINATION AT THE LAST MINUTE?

Examples of this are the students' protest in Tiananmen Square, Beijing and Albanian uprisings in Yugoslavia, both in the summer of 1989. Is it wise to travel? The Travel Advice Unit, run by the Consular Department of the Foreign and Commonwealth Office (see p 138) answers enquiries from the public about volatile situations such as these. Take their advice.

WHAT IF THERE IS ILLNESS IN THE FAMILY WHILE WE ARE TOURING ABROAD IN THE CAR?

Urgent messages are broadcast, courtesy of the BBC and Radio Luxembourg in the case of real emergencies. Before you go, leave background information, even a rough itinerary, with a motoring organisation such as the AA or the RAC. Obviously you should leave with someone at home the telephone number of all the places where you know you are staying and when.

These two examples are among the worst possible scenarios. They may help to put other anxieties into perspective.

KEEPING IN TOUCH WITH HOME

However far away friends and family may seem, they are really only a phone call away. For the occasional reassuring chat, it will usually be easier for you to phone them, rather than the other way round. Telephoning from a hotel can cost up to five times more than from a phone box. *Phoning the UK from Abroad* is a useful leaflet, obtainable from British Telecom (see p 143). It gives full and detailed information about ringing the UK, from a variety of different countries. It also lists cheap rates and time differences, and explains how many local phone boxes work. The following points are of particular note.

♦ International Direct Dialling is the fastest, cheapest way to place a call, and in many countries you can now buy slot-in phone cards which means you don't have to keep feeding the machine with coins.

♦ You can make reverse-charge calls without cash. This costs more, of course, but it may be convenient.

♦ If you have a British Telecom credit card you can use it to make calls via the international operator. The cost will appear on your next bill. Details of charges for credit-card calls are shown in a price list available at district offices. Again, these calls cost more, but you may find the method convenient.

In spite of telephone contact with family and friends, there may well be some aspects of British life that you will miss. In many resorts and cities there are church services in English and details of these can be obtained before you go from an organisation called Christians Abroad (see p 134). Even if you are not a regular churchgoer, the English church can be a meeting point for many of the local British community. Another way to keep in touch with home is by reading British newspapers, which are on sale in most resorts and cities. You could also consider using a short-wave radio to listen to the BBC World Service (see p 136).

A LAST WORD

If you are still having nervy, second thoughts prior to your departure, in spite of conscientious and thorough planning, then try to counter them with some positive thinking. There is a lot of preparation necessary for a long-stay holiday abroad; it amounts to a big investment in terms of time and energy. You have completed a great deal of background research, but that store of knowledge may prove to be the basis of many more holidays to come. The rewards of all your efforts should be evident after a few months. You will have returned from your long stay abroad, probably enriched and exhilarated, probably happy to be back home and, perhaps – after a few months have elapsed – ready for more!

4

Living Abroad

The right move?

HOW PERMANENT IS 'PERMANENT'?

Many people say that they plan to live abroad 'in their retirement', as though this period of their lives were a constant, unchanging time which they intend spending under blue skies. The truth of the matter is that retirement can span many years and no one can expect to feel the same way about things in their early 60s, as they do in their late 70s. There is no need for an arrangement to live abroad to be permanent, that is, until the end of your days. It can be 'permanent' for just as long as fits in with your personal plans, (bearing in mind, of course, that the best-made plans can be overturned by unforeseen events beyond our control).

Keeping your options open is highly recommended. There is a lot to be said for living abroad in Phase One of your retirement, the active years, and then returning to the UK in time for Phase Two. One possible weakness in this scheme is that few people recognise or, perhaps, acknowledge the gradual onset of Phase Two. Very often, they delay their return home until it is too late, and underestimate the stress and worry involved in resettling after a few years' absence.

A sensible approach, especially if Europe is your destination, is to plan living abroad for a *set* period only: say for two, three or even five years, depending on your circumstances. Setting yourselves a time limit, however flexible, gives you a clearly defined context for plans and decisions. Your return to the UK is integrated into the overall plan from the start, and adds impetus to the effort involved in staying in touch. This concept of a fixed-term stay has already been developed in Australia with their 'extended-stay retiree' scheme, where successful applicants with independent means can settle for a probationary period of four years (see p 98).

LOCATION

When you have retired, many 'established' restrictions no longer apply and you should be able to choose more freely where you would like to live. Many people tend to be drawn back to places they have known in the past. Whatever the sentiments behind your choice, your experience of your destination should be recent and up to date. Places can change beyond recognition in a relatively short time. Somewhere which was a happy holiday location is not necessarily the best choice for a semi-permanent home. You may need to explore the area further afield before finding the ideal location, which may prove to be no more than a few kilometres away. Just as when you are considering a move within the UK, it helps to define your needs quite specifically, analysing carefully your preferred lifestyle, interests and your family ties.

Many people choose to live in a European country because Europe is near and relatively convenient. You may well have been visiting different parts of it all your life. The whole business of travelling abroad can then feel like a natural and logical progression, starting with short-stay summer breaks, developing to long-stay holidays in the low season and then finally to living abroad on a semi-permanent basis. Another advantage to settling in Europe is the fact that it is obviously easier to keep in touch with home, family and friends.

Europe may be on the doorstep, but there are strong arguments too for choosing an English-speaking country; Australia, Canada, the US and South Africa are all possible choices for retired people with independent means. As a useful introduction and a source of contact, you could subscribe to one of the monthly newspapers intended for potential settlers and visitors. They are *Australasian News*, *Canada News* and *South Africa News*, all published by Outward Bound Newpapers (see p 143). Of course, the fact that English is a common language does not automatically guarantee your compatability with another country's way of life. Much of the advice in this section is just as relevant to English-speaking countries as it is to Europe.

Whichever country you choose, it obviously makes sense to get to know the region before you decide to retire there. It also makes sense to live there for some months so that you are familiar with the all-year-round climate. Deciding how long this kind of trial period should be is rather like defining the ideal period for a trial marriage! Anything under six months is hardly realistic, and even during the six months that follow you may well be living in an atmosphere of a holiday or honeymoon, rather than in the daily routine of everyday life. This time, it is not just a matter of adapting and surviving for six months in a strange country – which can be an adventure in itself. Your future happiness and integration in local life will depend on your personal reaction to the place and the people. Do you really feel at home? Do you feel you could belong here? Ask yourself the following questions:

Are the local people friendly and helpful?

What is their attitude to 'foreigners' living in 'their' town?

Have you talked to people who have been retired there for some years?

How much food shopping and cooking have you done?

Have you had first-hand experience of local medical services?

To what extent have you travelled on local buses and trains?

Have you had your shoes mended, your watch repaired, your hair cut?

YOU AND YOUR PARTNER

Whereas many a partnership is revitalised in retirement, and sharing travel adventures can add a new and exciting dimension to a relationship, it has to be said that marital and relationship problems figure more prominently in retirement than is generally realised. 120,000 divorces occur in the over-60s age group every year. On retirement, couples may suddenly find themselves dependent on each other's company day after day, having previously had separate lives and well-defined roles, and they must learn to adjust to the new circumstances. This is one of the reasons why a preliminary adjustment period together at home is preferable to moving abroad *immediately* on retirement.

An uneasy partnership can founder under the added stress of a new language, a strange location, and the possible hazards of social isolation and loneliness. Another well-documented problem is becoming alcohol dependent, particularly if you move to the Continent, where wine and spirits are generally cheap. A couple of brandies with the morning coffee may be a pleasant habit for a local, but is not without risks for a newcomer to the continental way of life. We take support services for granted in the UK, but marriage counselling, self-help groups or just straightforward advice and information services will not be easily available abroad.

CAN YOU AFFORD IT?

Property abroad may seem temptingly cheap in comparison with house prices here in the UK. However, you are not just dealing with an affordable one-off purchase. Buying a house is one thing (see Chapter 5), but you are also tying yourself to additional new commitments, such as medical insurance, at a time when your income may be actually falling.

A stable income, which may be adequate in the UK, is exposed to risks beyond your control once you move abroad. Your retirement income is likely to be geared to increases in the UK cost of living. The rate of inflation in your chosen country abroad, however, may be rising far more rapidly than at home, and your income cannot possibly hope to keep pace. In addition, any income paid to you in sterling – your pension, for example – has to be converted into local currency. The fluctuation in the exchange rate is yet another factor beyond your control. What seemed like a perfectly adequate income on leaving the UK, may prove to be extremely restrictive within a short period of time. Accordingly, no decision about living abroad should ever be made without taking sound professional advice about your financial situation.

ABROAD IS DIFFERENT

Companies often send employees abroad to work on a long-term basis. Before they go, routine briefings are provided on the day-to-day life of the particular country in question in order to smooth the way for such employees and their families. This background information, concerning things like shop opening hours, how the telephones work or how to find a doctor or dentist, etc is based on the fundamental truth that abroad is different. Foreigners have to learn to fit in. Retired Britons are no different. If you don't try to adapt when you live abroad, you may never be entirely happy.

—— *A British villa-owner* on the Costa Blanca reports, 'I've seen a number of people move out to Spain and Portugal and get increasingly frustrated because things aren't done in the same way as in the UK. They seem to forget that it is they who are the foreigners and it is they who have to accustom themselves to living in a foreign country.

'Life in Spain can be very frustrating. Getting a phone is a long-winded business. The electrical system and the water supply are unreliable. The post system is totally chaotic. The banking system is a nightmare to those used to the incredibly efficient system (comparatively speaking) that operates in the UK. Dealing with the Spanish bureaucracy can be a very frustrating experience for those used to dealing with (by and large) British officials. The people who make a satisfactory move are those who are relaxed to start with. You have to accept a great many of the frustrations and learn to accept the, for example, Spanish way of doing things. There's always tomorrow.'

As a retired person, without the support of a big business personnel or welfare department, where can you go for information and assistance?

♦ You can subscribe, as an individual, to a briefing series such as *Outlines for Expatriates*, produced by a publishing company called Employment Conditions Abroad (see p 142). The coverage is comprehensive in scope and is available for 70 countries. Much of the material relates to daily living.

♦ The Woman's Corona Society (see p 139) publishes a series called *Notes for Newcomers* and also runs one-day courses in London for both men and women. There are branches which welcome newcomers in many countries.

♦ Abroad, the English-speaking church serves a social as well as a religious need. The Anglican church has a network spanning most countries and will link newcomers to an on-the-spot contact already familiar with the area who will share his or her knowledge of the locality. A leaflet on overseas settlement is available.

ACCOMMODATION: TO RENT OR TO BUY?

You can live abroad on a semi-permanent basis quite comfortably without ever buying your own property. Home ownership is much more a way of life in the UK than in some other European countries, where families often hold long leases on apartments and villas.

Renting has a number of important advantages:

It gives you the opportunity to move from location to location with greater ease.

It can make the whole process of moving abroad easier and less long-winded. Also, when you decide to return to the UK, you will not have the problem of selling your property.

You have the chance to evaluate living abroad before committing yourself to a property purchase.

It gives you time to look round at leisure for just the right property to purchase.

Renting 'buys' time in one sense; on the other hand, if purchasing a property is your ultimate intention, property prices do not stay static. Advice on buying a property abroad is given in the last chapter of this book.

The availability of rented accommodation, furnished and unfurnished, varies. Mobility of housing is not as common as it is here. Away from tourist areas and in some capital cities, it may be more difficult to find and the rents may be higher. Estate agents do exist abroad but are generally not as prevalent as they are in the UK. A good place to look for accommodation is in local newspapers, where prospective landlords advertise their properties. Alternatively, you could put your own advertisement in the local English-language newspaper, or use the personal contact network, such as the noticeboard in the English church. In a tourist area, try the local regional tourist office for accommodation lists, as you would for a long-stay holiday (see p 34).

Before you go, the consular department in the UK may offer advice on finding accommodation. How to find rented accommodation may be included in a briefing series such as *Outlines for Expatriates*, already mentioned (see p 142).

Another possibility is the Air Travel Advisory Bureau (see p 136) a data system, which in addition to news on discounted flights, also supplies 'daily living' information about different countries. This is a telephone service and if you don't want to hold while the data comes up on the operator's screen, you can leave your name and address and they will send you details of any relevant accommodation agencies.

YOUR PROPERTY IN THE UK

There are strong arguments to retain a base in the UK if you decide to live abroad; some are set out below.

♦ Having a comfortable home available to you when you return to the UK will make the resettlement process easier and more congenial. You may not feel up to househunting as soon as you get back.

♦ If you sell your house and simply go abroad, you may find yourself unable to afford a similar property on your return. House prices may have risen disproportionately in the UK.

♦ You may be relying on an available room in the home of a married son or daughter. This is not always a good idea; families grow in size as well as in number and even a short period of, say, two years can see a lot of changes. Most families do not have surplus accommodation; sooner or later 'your' room may be needed for something else. Equally, it may be that living with your family would suit neither you nor your relatives: you never know how well you will get on until you actually live together.

If you do decide to retain a UK base while you are abroad, it is unlikely that you would want it to remain empty for the whole time. It is always preferable for buildings to be inhabited; it keeps the place warm and well-aired and reduces the risk of burglary or squatting. You may like to consider letting your property for the time that you are away.

Since the recent Housing Act was passed, owner-occupiers are now able to let their property in the confidence that tenants should move

out when required. Two sorts of tenancy agreement are possible. They are:
- **An assured shorthold tenancy**
- **An assured tenancy**

An assured shorthold tenancy

An assured shorthold tenancy empowers the landlord to recover the property on the date agreed for the end of the lease, or – in the case of a month-by-month agreement – by giving two months' notice. The initial let must be for a minimum of six months.

An assured tenancy

An assured tenancy gives security of tenure to the tenant, except in certain cases such as when the owner-occupier serves a document called a 'Ground 1 notice' before any agreement has been signed. This Ground 1 notice can be in the form of a letter stating that you may wish to repossess your property at the end of the agreed term. With this sort of tenancy there is no need for the initial let to be for six months.

Remember that unforeseen circumstances (such as illness, the death of a partner or just general disenchantment) may result in your returning to the UK earlier than anticipated. This is something to bear in mind when considering whether or not to let your property. You may opt for shorter rather than more long-term lets. You would also be wise to discuss with a financial advisor how letting your house might affect your tax position (see p 102).

If you decide to let your house it is essential to talk the matter over with a solicitor before drawing up either kind of tenancy agreement, although legal stationers are now producing DIY tenancy packs. The law stationers Oyez sell both assured shorthold and assured tenancy packs (see p 138). The important Ground 1 notice is a document which you have to write yourself.

In connection with letting your property, you may be interested in reading *Renting and Letting: The Legal Rights and Duties of Landlords and Tenants*, a handbook published by the Consumers' Association (see p 142).

MAINTAINING CONTACT

People who live abroad usually manage to maintain family ties through phone calls, letters and visits. Visits are often a one-way affair with plenty of younger relatives coming over to enjoy a holiday at your new home in the sun! However, it is important to maintain other personal connections too. Try not to lose touch with old friends; you will be glad of their company if you do eventually return to the UK.

In addition to your friends, there are a couple of professional contacts that you should maintain. Keep in touch with your financial advisor, perhaps twice a year, concerning any investments or tax queries. Keep in contact with a solicitor, too; you may occasionally require legal advice.

On a broader scale, it is prudent to keep abreast of social and political changes going on in the UK and around you. It is very easy to detach yourself from society when you live abroad. Time passes, things change, and without due care you may find yourself out of tune with the way most people think and act. A resident journalist on the Costa Blanca described the local, long-established community of British expatriates as 'a little piece of England in the sun; a place where time stands still – somewhere before the 1950s. The only regret of most of the British community here is that Spain is inhabited by Spaniards.' These sad survivors are trapped in their own time warp, incapable of integrating with the local community, but equally incapable of adjusting to life in the UK of the 1990s.

The most obvious and easiest way to keep in touch with current events is through the media, via:

Newspapers
Radio
Television

Newspapers

You can buy newspapers from the UK in most towns in Europe. They are usually a day late and cost the equivalent of about £1. In the capital and some main cities, there will be a branch of the British Council (see p 136), with a library and reading rooms containing UK newspapers and journals. In addition to reading the occasional daily paper, you may like to subscribe to a weekly 'potted' issue, prepared by *The Guardian*, called *The Guardian Weekly*, which aims to include the best articles of the previous six days as well as occasional pieces from the *Washington Post* and *Le Monde*. Alternatively, the *Financial Times* produces a monthly magazine for expatriates called *Resident Abroad* and you may like to subscribe to this (see p 142).

Radio

In northern France, and occasionally in parts of southern France and northern Spain, you can receive BBC radio on long wave (198kHz). For part of the day, you may also receive the BBC World Service on medium wave (648kHz). To receive the World Service on a continuous basis, you will need a shortwave receiver. The BBC uses as many as eight separate frequencies in one day, so radios with pre-set tuning buttons and direct tuning are the most convenient; they are also the most expensive. A mains adaptor is usually supplied with the small portable radios on the market and this avoids the expense of batteries. The aerial on the radio is usually sufficient for good reception, although in steelframe buildings such as high-rise hotels or apartment blocks the best reception will be on the balcony. You may like to subscribe to *London Calling*, a monthly magazine put out by the BBC giving full details of World Service programmes and frequencies.

You may be interested to call at the BBC World Service shop at Bush House where there is a range of recommended short wave receivers on display and also a collection of books on short wave radio and satellite TV. Alternatively you can send for their book list (see p 136).

Television

Local television is useful not only for the news but also for acquiring additional familiarity with the language. You can invariably understand a foreign language better than you can speak it. TV presenters speak clearly and are excellent tutors for pronunciation and for demonstrating the ebb and flow of the language. Watch out, too, for English and American films with sub-titles in the local language. This is another good way to deepen your understanding of the language.

If you have a video recorder, you may be interested in subscribing to BBC Video World (see p 136), a fortnightly cassette service compiled from the best of the output from BBC1 and BBC2. Every two weeks, subscribers receive a three-hour tape including current affairs, sport, and a selection of comedy, drama and documentaries. Tapes can be supplied in the format appropriate to your machine, wherever you live.

WHEN TO RETURN

The timing of your return to the UK should ideally be part of an overall strategy, which takes into account your individual financial and tax position. This is why it is vital to retain access to professional advice during your years abroad. (Keeping up to date with recent changes in legislation which may affect investments and tax is a necessary part of retirement planning, whether or not you live abroad.)

Unfortunately, many expatriates delay their return to the UK until they are too old and frail to cope on their own. Age Concern, and other similar agencies, are at the receiving end of many sad letters and requests for help from people who have grown old abroad and who are totally out of touch with, say, UK housing conditions. There is a scarcity of 'extra care' accommodation and rented sheltered housing, and there are long waiting lists for whatever accommodation the councils and housing associations have available.

Quite apart from the question of finance and suitable accommodation, many people greatly underestimate the energy and effort involved in setting up home again in the UK. Re-creating a lifestyle which is comfortable, interesting and satisfying under grey skies needs a significant input of enthusiasm and effort. A spell of life in the sun is a hard act to follow.

—— **Eileen Chapman**, a widow in her early 70s, returned to this country four years ago to look after her father, who has since died. This was not a planned return, but Eileen has subsequently realised the advantages of moving back while she is still sufficiently active to make the necessary and demanding adaptations. She enjoyed life abroad, working as a secretary in Athens and in Paris, and has found it difficult to settle in the suburbia of southeast England. 'When you live abroad, you feel you're an international person. You come home and you're a national person all over again and it isn't easy.'

Thanks to her adaptability and resourcefulness, Eileen has been able to cope with the problems she has faced of housing, loneliness and bureaucracy. Fortunately, she was able to stay on in her father's flat, which is owned by a housing association; a private landlord might not have been so sympathetic. Without sufficient capital, Eileen stood no chance of becoming a first-time buyer, particularly in this expensive area.

Eileen finds that opportunities for companionship and meeting other people are limited. Although she has attended adult education classes and joined in local activities, friendships take time to develop. 'Life is much more open in other countries. People meet outside more, in cafes and restaurants. It's all much more casual and informal. People here tend to live behind closed doors. My sister-in-law couldn't understand why I hadn't got any friends here. What she didn't realise was that all my friends were abroad somewhere else, miles away. You lose touch with English friends over the years. It's hard to pick up again after a long gap, and it takes a while to make new friends. It doesn't happen overnight.'

One difference Eileen has found on her return to the UK is a marked increase in bureaucracy. 'At least abroad you can go to whichever doctor you choose. Here I got put on the same list as my father, and there I'm stuck. It seems impossible to change to a doctor I can actually talk to.' This quirk of the UK healthcare system is just one example of how infuriating the petty difficulties of everyday life can be to someone unused to the system. It is a reminder, too, that life in the UK is not all roses!

Eileen often feels nostalgic for the life she lived abroad, but she does admit that memory is selective: 'You forget about the insects and the cockroach powder in little heaps all over the house. And the dreadful water shortages. You remember the best bits.'

Your status at home and abroad

Just as you have to tackle the planning and preparation before a long-stay holiday, so you have to tie up a great many loose ends in the UK before you actually move abroad on a semi-permanent basis. Information is more easily and, perhaps, more quickly available here. If you have tried an experimental long-stay holiday you may know the language and the systems; consequently, looking up addresses and finding telephone numbers should take less time and trouble. You will know several sources where you can check information.

While you make your preparations, try to form the habit of thinking a few years ahead. If, for example, you are under age for a State retirement pension, check with the DSS that you have a full contribution record. If not, it will be in your own interests to 'top it up' with voluntary contributions (see p 100). There may well be a period of unemployment or some other gap long ago that you have forgotten about.

Make sure that any information you acquire is based on your individual circumstances and is from an official source. Do not act on the hearsay experience of other retired people. Although they may appear to share a similar situation to your own, their background circumstances are bound to be different from yours. Alternatively, their experience may be out of date and the regulations may have changed.

The guidelines in this book concerning requirements and

regulations are signposts only to encourage you to find out as much as you can by reading the relevant books and leaflets on all the aspects involved in living abroad. Regulations, both in the UK and abroad, are subject to frequent changes, particularly as 1992 approaches.

RESIDENCY REQUIREMENTS

Initial enquiries concerning residence abroad should be made in the UK to the consular or immigration department of the country concerned (see p 139). Procedures differ from country to country. Applications for European countries are usually made in person and can take several months. Progress is made in stages starting with visas and followed by extensions and renewals, according to the regulations, until full resident status is granted. By this time, of course, you may already be living in the country as a tourist or visitor, endorsed by the appropriate visa or permit. You may already own property there.

Before countries will give you resident status, there are a number of conditions you have to fulfil. These include:

sufficient income to support yourself;

private medical insurance;

confirmation of accommodation.

The consular department to which you made your application will inform you which documents are required as evidence of these.

Under proposed new EC legislation, retired people from the UK and all other member countries will have right of residence anywhere within the EC, on proof of pension (or other income) and medical insurance. This proposal is causing considerable controversy in some EC countries and a counterproposal, containing a number of restrictions, is currently under discussion.

Another sensitive area within the EC is employment. Although unrestricted mobility of labour is the intention, in practice this is still a long way off. As a retired person, you may well have stated in your permanent residence application that you did not intend to seek work. However, it may happen that you will be offered some part-time employment – translation work, or a consultancy arrangement, perhaps. Be careful here. Take great care not to endanger your residency status by failing to observe local regulations, however petty or annoying they may seem. Some part-time work may well be a possibility, but seek professional advice. Should you, in due course, wish to set up your own small business, you must observe local regulations. Again, request professional advice on how to do this.

The requirements for retiring to Australia under their 'extended-stay retiree' provisions demand sufficient funds to maintain yourself. The levels set as 'sufficient funds' are high: capital for transfer of at least A$500,000 (£250,000), or a minimum capital for transfer of A$150,000 (£75,000), which is deemed your 'establishment cost', plus a pension or other annual income of over A$35,000 (£17,500). Extended-stay retirees are not covered by Medicare, Australia's healthcare system, so need to take out private medical and hospital healthcare cover. There must be no intention of entering the workforce. These conditions of entry are at least comparable to those in force in other countries like the US, Canada and New Zealand.

Retired people without independent means who wish to join relatives in Australia, New Zealand or Canada may be considered under the various family schemes which are organised in those countries. They involve 'sponsorship' by a younger relative who is already resident in the country. It is important that all the family members who are involved in this kind of family scheme understand fully and accept the significance of sponsorship: namely that an assurance of support is promised which includes the provision of accommodation. Not every retired person would want that degree of dependency on relatives. Advice leaflets for parents who wish to emigrate can be obtained from immigration departments either within the relevant country or in the UK (see p 139). British immigrants are, of course, subject to the same regulations affecting all prospective immigrants and these are subject to change from time to time.

SOCIAL SECURITY AND HEALTH CARE

Before leaving the UK on a semi-permanent basis, you will need to review your situation regarding the following:

Benefits

Pensions

Health care

Benefits

Inform the DSS Overseas Branch (see p 137) of your plans, well in advance of your departure. Tell them which benefits you are currently receiving, your intended destination and your National Insurance number. They are then in a position to provide you with individual information, according to your circumstances and your chosen country.

If you are going to an EC country you may be covered by their social security rules. See leaflet SA 29 *Your social security, health care and pension rights in the EC*, available from any DSS office.

If you are going to a country which has a reciprocal agreement with the UK, the Overseas Branch of the DSS will send you the appropriate leaflet. These countries include Australia, the US, Canada, Malta, New Zealand, Jamaica, and others. A full list is contained in the leaflet NI 38 *Social security abroad*, available from any DSS office.

Pensions

Retirement and widows' pensions can be paid to you anywhere abroad, no matter how long you are away. Inform your DSS office well in advance so that arrangements can be made for paying your pension to any one of the following:

your address abroad every four or thirteen weeks;

your UK bank, building society or National Savings Bank account;

a person of your choice who lives in the UK;

a bank account abroad.

Outside the EC you will only receive annual increases in your pension if you are living in a country which has an agreement with the UK. These countries are: Austria, Bermuda, Cyprus, Finland, Gibraltar, Guernsey, Iceland, Israel, Jamaica, Jersey, Malta, Mauritius, Sark, Sweden, Switzerland, Turkey, the US and Yugoslavia. If you live anywhere else, your pension will be frozen at the amount it was when you left the UK. You will receive the current, higher rate of pension on your return.

If you have retired early and are going to live abroad, you will be able to claim your State retirement pension when you reach the statutory age (65 for men, 60 for women). Before you depart, it would be wise to request a pension forecast, as a check that you have a full contribution record. Ask for Form BR 19 at the DSS office. There is no obligation to pay contributions if you are resident abroad, but it may be in your own interest to pay Class 3 voluntary contributions, particularly if you live in an EC country. This can be done with a single yearly payment via a British bank.

Health care

A word of warning here. Do not assume, like many people who go to live abroad, that you can always return to the UK for any serious operation that might prove necessary. This is not the case. Leaflet NI 38 explains: 'As a general rule, if you return on a visit to the UK, you will not get free treatment if the purpose of your visit is to get medical treatment.' In other words, while you may get the treatment, you will also get the bill! Should you have an accident, however, or fall ill while on a visit to the UK, you would probably qualify for free treatment as an emergency. When you return to live in the UK, you will again be eligible for free NHS treatment.

Private medical insurance is a common condition of granting residence abroad. In choosing a policy suitable for your needs, there are a few points to consider.

♦ Your insurance should include repatriation in the case of serious illness or injury.

- It should provide cover for you to be moved to the nearest centre of medical excellence.

- It should cover dental treatment.

In some Mediterranean countries, no matter how good your insurance cover is, it can be very difficult to find health services of the standard you are used to in the UK. Unlike the NHS primary care system, where GPs are available for free consultation daily and by appointment, similar clinics abroad may be held for just one hour a day, very early in the morning, and on a 'first-come-first-served' basis.

You may like to refer to the section on health care in Chapter 3 *Long-stay holidays: getting ready to go* which deals with medical check-ups before leaving the UK (see p 56). If you are taking prescription tablets on a regular basis for blood pressure, angina, etc you will need an introduction to a local doctor shortly after arrival in order to ensure a continuation of supplies. Ideally, a previous stay in the locality will have already provided the opportunity to find a local doctor. Alternatively, you could ask another English-speaking resident or the local pharmacy to recommend a doctor. A letter from your GP in the UK, giving the dosage and generic name of the drug you are taking, might smooth the way.

Until such time as you can check on the local availability of over-the-counter supplies, such as batteries for hearing aids or cleansing solution for contact lenses, you will need to take a supply with you. These items may be available locally, but probably at a higher price. They are the kind of items that friends could bring when they visit you.

YOUR TAX POSITION

Perhaps the first thing to say here is that you should seek professional advice on the implication of foreign residence on your tax situation *before* you leave the UK. The exact timing of your departure can make a considerable difference to your tax bill. The whole area of taxation both at home and abroad is extremely complex and the guidance given here cannot hope to take into account the different regulations that apply to individual circumstances. However, for the interested reader, background information is supplied regarding:

UK tax

Foreign tax

UK tax

For anyone who is emigrating (that is, selling up their home and leaving the UK for good), the situation is relatively simple. You notify the Inland Revenue of your intentions by filling in Form P85; this includes a claim for any outstanding money which may be due to you. If, however, you are planning to live in Europe, keep close links with the UK and retain a base here, the situation is far from simple. You should seek individual professional advice since your tax situation, both here and abroad, your savings and investments, and your income are all closely inter-related. You should particularly seek information on your liability for the community charge (poll tax).

Many British people, who live abroad and who retain a UK home, have to wait three years after their departure before it can be established whether they are resident or non-resident for UK tax purposes. A provisional-only assessment by the Inland Revenue makes any sort of sensible financial planning for retirement extremely difficult. Professional advice is vital.

Statutory guidance is lacking. The best available is the booklet IR 20 *Residents' and Non-Residents' Liability to Tax in the UK*, a copy of which can be obtained from the Inland Revenue Public Enquiry Room at Somerset House. Other useful reading is Allied Dunbar's *Expatriate Tax and Investment Guide* (see p 142) and *Retiring Abroad*, published by the Financial Times (see p 142).

As the rules stand, the position is this. If you live abroad, you are deemed a tax resident in the UK if you do any one of the following:

spend six months (183 days) or more in the UK per year (and this means the April-to-April tax year);

make habitual and substantial visits of at least three months' (90 days') duration, measured over a period of four years;

visit the UK, for however short a time, and have accommodation available for your use.

Needless to say, it is the last rule, regarding available accommodation, which is the most frequent source of dispute, particularly as there is no apportionment of the year into periods of residence and non-residence. A visit to the UK lasting one day in order to attend a funeral is sufficient cause to deem you a resident for the whole of that tax year, if available accommodation exists for your use – *even if you don't make use of it*. If your UK home is let on a long lease, then that accommodation will not be *available* for your use. It is the *availability* of the accommodation, not the actual ownership, which is significant to the taxman. A room in a relative's house, reserved solely for your use, would count as 'available accommodation'.

Recent proposals to clarify the rules for determining residence and to scrap the accommodation rule have not yet been acted on, but they would greatly simplify the situation for many retired people who want the safeguard of retaining a UK base.

However, in many cases, double taxation agreements exist and can determine in which country a person or a particular source of income is to be taxed. These agreements prevent you from paying tax on the same income both abroad and in the UK. Certain types of income (eg occupational pensions, dividends, interest received on a range of Government securities, etc) are taxable in one country, while other income may be taxable in the other. These arrangements vary from country to country. Government pensions (eg for teachers, members of the Armed Services, the NHS, etc) are always taxable in the UK.

The double taxation agreements mainly cover income tax. Where inheritance or capital gains tax is concerned, you should seek professional advice.

Foreign tax

Generally, owning property in another country makes you liable for tax, whether you live there or not. There are property taxes as a result of buying (or selling), and also annual taxes, which are due as a result of ownership and/or letting your home, if this applies. Allied Dunbar's Money Guides contain very clear and concise explanations of how the individual tax systems work in certain countries. Titles include *Your Home in France*, *Your Home in Italy*, *Your Home in Portugal* and *Your Home in Spain* (see p 142).

The most significant difference between the tax authorities abroad and those in the UK is that, abroad, the onus is on the individual to comply and pay taxes promptly, without being chased by letter. You will not necessarily be notified of tax that is due, but failing to pay up on time can result in fines. Pay now, argue later should be your rule. It is a good idea to employ a local accountant who will obviously be familiar with the system. In fact, in Spain it is now obligatory for a non-resident property owner to appoint a fiscal representative and to have a fiscal identification number.

Misunderstandings and failure to pay local taxes can have quite serious repercussions. To quote Spain again, where tax evasion used to be much more widespread than it is now, unpaid taxes are registered by the authorities as a debt. Unpaid debts are liable to fines, which can accumulate, often unknown to the inadvertent defaulter, whose first indication that something is amiss may be finding his or her name listed in an official bulletin of debtors! The easiest way to recover debt from foreigners is to seize their property, which is what the authorities sometimes do in extreme cases. One of the services offered by a UK self-help organisation – the International Property Owners Organisation (see p 137) is the publication in its magazine of the official list of debtors in Spanish tourist areas. They will also investigate the reasons why a member's name appears in the bulletin. The organisation also acts as a pressure group and is currently trying to persuade the Spanish authorities to translate official information regarding taxes on foreign-owned property into other languages.

Living in another country means you may be considered a 'tax resident'. Different countries have different rules about this but they are usually based on the proportion of the year a person spends in that country. In Spain and Portugal, for example, residency for a period of six months (183 days) or more renders you liable for tax. Because of the anomaly in the dates of a tax year – January to December in most of Europe, April to April in the UK – it is possible to be a tax resident in two countries at once! Double taxation agreements ensure you will not be taxed twice on the same income. It is worth noting here that under the new rules of the Organisation for Economic Co-operation and Development (OECD), there is now a great deal of interchange of information between countries, and tax debts owing in one country can be followed up in another.

Consult a professional if inheritance tax is likely to apply while you are abroad because the laws governing inheritance are extremely complex.

Moving arrangements

Moving your home overseas is obviously a major undertaking which requires careful thought and planning. Your criteria are likely to vary according to whether or not you choose to retain a UK base and consequently a place where you can store items you do not wish to take with you. In certain circumstances it can prove cheaper to buy 'new' when you reach your destination rather than paying to have bulky goods shipped abroad; this can include car purchase. All the appropriate options should be carefully considered before any decisions are taken.

REMOVALS

The process of packing cannot even begin until a great deal of sifting and sorting has been done. Normally when you are moving house, you can afford to be lenient about packing odd items you are not sure about; often an occasional piece of furniture, previously relegated to the loft, will find a nice little niche in the new home. Not so this time. Sentimentality is a luxury you will have to pay for. This is going to be the most expensive move you are ever likely to make!

You cannot move abroad without paperwork – lots of it – including export licences, import licences and all the other documentation involved with shipping and customs clearance. Where do you begin?

There is a free leaflet, *Your Keys to Moving Abroad*, available from the British Association of Removers (BAR), which is a good place to start (see p 136). After that, you need to get in touch with a specialist removal firm, ideally one that belongs to BAR's Overseas Group, because you will then be guaranteed a door-to-door removal, carried out via their links with a similarly reputable removal company in your country of destination. Always obtain estimates from a few UK firms before making your final choice. Many overseas removal firms, such as Pickfords, have open days when potential customers can see for themselves what practical arrangements are made for their furniture and possessions.

Specialist removal firms are most likely to know the ropes and are in a position to advise you on a wide variety of queries. For example, you may be unsure whether certain items of furniture are worth transporting. Would it be cheaper to buy 'new' abroad? A specialist firm will know that locally made furniture is often preferable, particularly in countries where the humidity is significantly different from in the UK. Such firms should also be in a position to advise on storage facilities in the UK.

Specialist firms can also help with fumigation. You may be unaware that the authorities in some countries insist on certain items of furniture (eg cane furniture, and mattresses) being fumigated or steam-cleaned, and at your expense! Your removal firm can undertake this for you.

Before your goods are packed up, there is one piece of paperwork that you will have to do yourself: a complete inventory of every single item, one copy for yourself and the other for the remover. This can help prevent delays through customs. Most household goods are shipped, and customs clearance takes about ten days to two weeks. You will be contacted regarding a delivery date of the furniture to your new home, although goods can be stored if necessary.

If your new home is already furnished, or if you are letting your

UK home, then you may only need overseas transport solely for your books and personal effects. Nevertheless, this too is a specialist removal job; your goods are packed up in a lightweight carton and the firm again guarantees door-to-door delivery. Avoid the cut-price alternative of a firm that transports your goods just from the house to the UK port; this not only leaves your goods stranded at customs, it leaves you stuck with all the problems of arranging clearance, transfer arrangements and delivery to your new home.

Most international removers require customers to settle their account before their goods leave the country. The BAR Overseas Group belongs to a protection scheme called the International Movers Mutual Insurance (IMMI) which is another safeguard for its customers; it guarantees a complete refund should any member company fail to fulfil its commitments.

ELECTRICAL AND CONSUMER GOODS

Some of the larger electrical items in your home will need special consideration – for a variety of reasons – before you pay to have them moved abroad.

♦ Electric cookers and heaters may not be compatible with local electricity supplies, or they may not work efficiently. You may have to buy new ones.

♦ If you intend living in a more rural area, away from large shops, consider whether you will need a larger fridge/freezer.

♦ Your existing TV set may not be convertible for local reception. It could be useful, however, if used with a video recorder, for playing videotapes recorded in the UK, sent by friends or relatives.

Alternatively, there may be consumer items which it could be worth your while purchasing before you leave the UK. Buy and use these some months in advance of your departure to avoid queries at customs.

♦ A DIY enthusiast may like to stock up on a range of tools and equipment. The cheaper models of power tools are not easily found in Europe, for example, where only the more expensive, professional quality tools tend to be stocked.

♦ High quality garden tools, particularly those made of stainless steel and manufactured in the UK, are much cheaper here than abroad. They will not take up much of your valuable removal space.

Advice and information regarding the necessary export and import licences and procedures can be obtained from the appropriate consular office in the UK. Your most valuable source of advice, however, is again a specialist removal firm, whose representative will visit you in your own home.

PETS

Including your pet in your plans to live abroad needs careful consideration and you would be wise to seek advice from your vet. The majority of pets travel easily, but there can be problems. For example, older dogs may find a long journey very stressful, while any kind of elderly pet may fail to adapt to Mediterranean heat. If you are flying, pets make the journey in their own air travel containers in the pressurised hold of the aircraft. The containers come in over 50 sizes and are recommended by the RSPCA. You will need your pet's measurements: height, shoulder width and length (excluding tail) plus their approximate weight.

The specialist international removal firm which deals with the removal of your household effects will probably also be able to sub-contract the task of animal transportation to a reputable, specialist firm. Always ask for a quotation for this extra service. The pet specialist firm will be represented at any open day the removal company arranges, which is a good opportunity for pet owners to ask questions and allay any anxieties.

There is extra paperwork involved in transporting an animal from one country to another. Import regulations vary from country to country. Typical conditions which need to be met before admitting an animal into another country include:

a recent health certificate from a registered UK vet;

a minimal period in quarantine on arrival (usually a matter of days);

a rabies vaccination.

Enquiries regarding the requirements of individual countries should be made to the relevant consular office in London.

If your destination is France, your animal can travel with you by car on the ferry, provided you have the correct documentation. Things can get complicated if you are going on to Spain, where the documentation requirements are different. If you do not intend using the services of a removal firm (because you are going to furnished accommodation, perhaps) you may like to deal direct with a firm such as Airpets Oceanic (see p 136), which specialise in animal transportation and run a door-to-door courier service, if necessary.

It is worth remembering that any dog or cat returning to the UK from abroad has to spend six months in quarantine under the UK 1974 Rabies Act. EC regulations may relax this condition in time. You are allowed to visit your pet in quarantine kennels.

BUYING A CAR FOR OVERSEAS USE

As a visitor you can take a UK car abroad with only minimal modifications such as headlight adjustment. As a resident you need a car which complies with local vehicle regulations.

Earlier visits to the place where you intend living will have given you the opportunity to observe which cars – the makes and models – are popular with local residents. Take care to disregard the cars used by car-hire firms; these will be fleet purchases, not necessarily based on local sales and servicing facilities.

Two important factors which should influence your choice of car are the following.

♦ You want the distance between your new home and the local repair and service centre to be minimal. While car distributors are in the main towns only, smaller local garages are usually appointed as 'approved repair centres' for particular car manufacturers. No one wants to drive 80 kms for a routine service.

♦ Which fuel do you want to buy – diesel or petrol? A car which runs on diesel is cheaper to maintain. The car itself costs more to buy initially, but it will have a higher resale value, especially in countries like France or Spain, where diesel fuel is much cheaper than petrol. Fuel consumption becomes an even more important consideration when a car also has air conditioning.

Another factor to bear in mind is that the road surfaces will not always be as good as you are accustomed to, so avoid cars with a low ground clearance. Also, parking a big car is going to cause problems in the narrow streets and alleys of small continental towns, which were certainly not planned with today's traffic in mind.

When you have finally settled on the car of your choice, you need to decide where and how to buy it. There are three main options.

♦ You can purchase the car in the UK to the specificaion of your country of destination, under the personal export scheme. This entitles you to up to six months' use of the car before leaving the UK and the price is free of car tax and VAT. The UK export office of the relevant car manufacturer can supply details and make all necessary arrangements. In addition to the savings you make in the UK, you may be able to take advantage of tax concessions on the personal import of cars in your country of destination – but these will be phased out eventually within the EC. An advantage of buying your car in the UK is that you will be able to drive it to your new home and take any items immediately needed on arrival.

♦ You can order the car in the UK through the export office of the manufacturer and collect it in your new country of residence.

♦ You can order your new car abroad from a local distributor. Allow up to three months if you want a specific model or colour since local agents do not usually hold large stocks.

You will have to make advance insurance arrangements that meet local regulations. Some countries insist that third-party insurance cover is provided by local companies but allow other risks (eg fire, theft or accidental damage to your own car) to be covered by insurance companies outside the country. Your existing insurers may have associates abroad, and by asking them to arrange cover you may retain some of your no-claims bonus. Fully-comprehensive car insurance can cost up to 100 per cent more than in the UK; a small compensation is the fact that vehicle tax for most small cars tends to be lower than in the UK. Vehicle tax should be obtained when the car is registered. Unlike the UK's centralised system, vehicle registration in Europe is organised on a regional basis.

Returning to the UK

AN UNFORESEEN RETURN

There is always the possibility when you go to live abroad that you may have to return sooner than you had originally intended. There are a variety of different reasons. Sadly, the death of a partner may be the cause. Another might be inadequate finance; people retiring at 55 may have decades of life on a pension ahead of them. It is difficult to forecast accurately the course of overseas inflation and exchange rates that far ahead. Financial advice is vital from the start.

Other people return sooner than expected because they just have not managed to settle. The demands of adjusting to such entirely new and different circumstances, all at once, may prove more than they can cope with. Additionally, they may be more homesick than they ever anticipated.

There is no reason whatever to feel depressed, ashamed or guilty that the great idea did not work out after all. The belief that the grass is greener on the other side of the fence is extremely widespread. Console yourself with the thought that it won't be the first mistake you have ever made in your life, and it probably won't be the last!

On the practical side, acknowledging the possibility of an emergency homecoming is vital *before* buying a home in another country. The resale possibilities of a house vary according to location and how much new property is being built in the area. Only the most saleable property makes sense for most people. Ask yourself whether your new home might be attractive to other potential second-home buyers in the UK (unless, that is, the next generation in your family is closely involved in the purchase and would be enthusiastic inheritors!)

DEATH ABROAD

In the event of a death – whatever the cause – the local British Consulate must be contacted immediately. The Consul will be able to advise you on special arrangements and can also play a useful role in informing next of kin. It is a useful precaution to make a note of the Consulate's address and phone number as soon as you arrive in case of any emergency although the local police should have this information. After normal office hours (local hours, that is), most British Consulates operate an answerphone service giving an alternative phone number in the event of an emergency.

A person's death should be registered with the British Consulate so that a record is kept in the UK at the General Register Office at St Catherine's House. You will be able to get a death certificate from the Consulate or, at a later date, St Catherine's House (see p 137).

It is a frequent requirement in hot countries for a burial or cremation to take place within one or two days of death. In view of this speed, it is sensible to acquaint yourself with local procedures on arrival in the country. These procedures vary from region to region within countries. Usually, there is one local undertaker for the area. Undertakers often expect payment for their services in cash.

You can arrange for a burial in a local cemetery or cremation. Cremation is not nearly so common overseas as it is in the UK and it tends to be more expensive, depending on local facilities. After a cremation you are able to transport the ashes back to the UK. If you wish to transport a body back to the UK for burial or cremation, you should be aware that it can cost between two and three thousand pounds, in addition to the eventual costs of the funeral back home. In order to transport a body in this way, you will need authorisation from a coroner or similar authority and, on arrival in the UK, you will be required to produce an authenticated translation of the foreign death certificate.

MAKING A WILL

If you die before you have made a Will, containing clear instructions on how you wish your assets to be handled, then the law steps in with its own intestacy rules. This is true in any country, but each country has its own laws about inheritance and inheritance tax and they are generally very different from those that operate in the UK.

You can include your foreign assets in your UK Will, but it will take time to verify matters at such a distance and is an added complication for your next of kin. A better course of action for anyone with property or assets overseas is to make an additional Will abroad, according to local laws and written in the local language. It is not obligatory to use the services of a lawyer, but it is highly advisable, particularly since your lawyer could also serve as your executor.

Needless to say, you will have to ensure that your foreign and UK Wills are compatible.

5

Buying a Property Abroad

A few warnings

The Costa Blanca (*Two sonnets*)

She: The Costa Blanca! Skies without a stain!
     Eric and I at almond blossom time
     Came here and fell in love with it. The climb
     Under the pine trees, up the dusty lane
     To Casa Kenilworth, brought me back again
     Our honeymoon, when I was in my prime.
     Goodbye democracy and smoke and grime;
     Eric retires next year. We're off to Spain.

     We've got the perfect site beside the shore,
     Owned by a charming Spaniard, Miguel,
     Who says that he is quite prepared to sell
     And build our Casa for us *and*, what's more,
     Preposterously cheaply. We have found
     Delightful English people living round.

He: (*five years later*)
     Mind if I see your *Mail*? We used to share
     Our *Telegraph* with people who've returned –
     The lucky sods! I'll tell you what I've learned.
     If you come out here put aside the fare
     To England, *I'd* run like a bloody hare
     If I'd a chance, and how we both have yearned
     To see our Esher lawn. I think we've earned
     A bit of what we had once over there.

     That Dago caught the wife and me all right!
     Here on this tideless tourist littered sea
     We're stuck. You'd hate it too if you were me:
     There's no piped water on the bloody site.
     Our savings gone, we climb the stony path
     Back to the house with scorpions in the bath.

                     John Betjeman

Does this sound far-fetched? Don't you believe it! John Betjeman managed to hit several nails on the head in this poem and, sadly, it accurately reflects the experience of many people who enthusiastically rush into buying property abroad, and who then repent at leisure.

Buying a home abroad doesn't have to be a miserable fiasco, *if* you take various sensible precautions, just as you would regarding any property purchase in this country. Perhaps the first thing to say is this: you do not have to buy. The section on page 33 deals with living in rented accommodation abroad, which is much more a way of life overseas, and can be a perfectly satisfactory arrangement. However, if you are committed to buying somewhere, then you should be aware of the potential problems, notably in relation to:

Property fraud and malpractice
Costs
Water
Telephones

Property fraud and malpractice

When Euro MP Edward McMillan-Scott investigated property fraud on behalf of the Ombudsman's Committee of the European Parliament, he drew particular attention to Spain. He quoted the string of illegal developments along both the Mediterranean and Atlantic coasts, where speculators had bought up agricultural land – which is cheaper than building land – and built on it in the hope of obtaining planning permission retrospectively. In fact, this permission was never forthcoming although plots were sold on the basis of permission being pending. Misguided buyers not only risked the appropriation of 'their' property, but also the refusal of the authorities to connect them to electricity, water and gas supplies.

Very often the speculators are not Spanish, but North Europeans – including some British. Under UK company law, a bankrupt company can be dissolved, leaving its creditors high and dry, while the directors resume business as usual the next day under a different name. Several recommendations have been made in the EC, in an attempt to deal with this kind of fraud and malpractice. Among them is the proposal for a centralised pool of information containing a European register with the names of all individuals who have been banned by court order from acting as the director of a company registered in any one of the member states.

Such changes lie in the future. In the meantime, victims must take their share of the blame for being shortsighted and greedy, for cutting corners and expecting an overseas home on the cheap.

—— **A British villa-owner** tells the following story: 'Every time I go to Spain I am faced with examples of the stupidity of people. The latest involved some land adjacent to my own property. An English businessman has paid £60,000 for the land and simply handed the cheque over without any consideration at all for the legal or financial niceties. He has little or no chance of getting his money back. He is, of course, shouting "fraud", but the reality is he is the victim of his own stupidity. If you had asked him to hand over £60,000 in this country for a plot of land, he wouldn't have made a move without talking to his solicitor. The last person he thought of talking to in Spain was a lawyer. Now it's too late.'

DIY property-buying in a foreign country, and this includes timeshare, is a risky business. What is quite astonishing is the way that many people heed dubious advice about 'how these things are done in Spain' (or elsewhere) from a relative stranger, perhaps a fellow Briton, whom they have recently met in a bar, rather than pay for professional advice from a British or local lawyer.

Costs

Most property abroad is cheaper than in the UK. Legal fees, however, are much higher, and there are taxes and registration fees of various kinds involved in property purchase. You will need to set aside 10-20 per cent of your agreed purchase budget to cover these fees in addition to a safety margin for fluctuating exchange rates.

If you are considering buying a newly-built house, you will need to know if the cost of connecting water, electricity and drainage is included in the selling price. You must also consider the running costs. Standing charges for water, electricity (and telephone, if you have one) will be payable, even if you are not there for six months of the year.

Repairs and maintenance are another cost factor. Exterior paintwork in particular needs frequent attention due to the effects of strong sunlight and drying winds. With an older property, you will have to arrange its upkeep yourself, and local labour may not be cheap. With a new development, maintenance may be included so check on the annual charge for this.

Do not rely on letting your property in order to make ends meet. In any case, letting may not be allowed under local regulations, or there may be certain conditions imposed, such as only letting through the local tourist office. Remember that any income you do make through letting your property will be subject to tax.

Water

This used to be a commodity that UK residents once took completely for granted. Now we all realise that clean, safe water does not just come out of the tap for free; processing, purifying and distribution all have to be paid for by some means or other. Not only that, but rarely, if ever, do we question the ready availability of water.

In Mediterranean countries, where it seldom rains in certain seasons and where the rainfall is not evenly distributed throughout the country as a whole, water supplies cannot be taken for granted. There may be plenty of water for baths and showers in the tourist hotels, but for local residents and property owners, water is metered and charged for according to usage, in addition to a standing charge. Also, there are often shortages and periods of time when the water may be cut off. No longer will you leave the tap running while you wash salads, rinse vegetables and clean your teeth!

Standards of water purity are higher in most EC countries than they are in the UK. However, no doubt the quality of water will vary. For nine months of the year there may be no problem, but in midsummer – at the time of peak demand – the water may be salty because it is drawn from a very low table. Bottled water is widely used.

When buying property, make enquiries about the local water supplies, preferably from local residents rather than the vendor. You may consider having your own water storage tank constructed, but this will require planning permission. In some areas the water may be very hard and you may consider installing a water softener.

Telephones

Having a private telephone installed, particularly in the rural areas of some countries, can mean waiting over a year. Public telephones are much more accessible than in the UK; there are many more in cafes and bars, as well as in the usual street kiosks. For more information on ringing the UK from abroad see page 80.

Sole ownership

DEFINING YOUR NEEDS

This is *your* retirement. Do not let property developers and estate agents, who are both anxious to cash in on the growing market for retirement homes abroad, define what is a suitable home for you. That is for you to work out and decide for yourself. There is much more to life in retirement than a perpetual holiday in the sun; that could get very boring day after day. You are an individual with your own interests, and this is to be *your* home, semi-permanent or otherwise.

The important question to ask yourself is what do you want from your property purchase abroad? Do you want an all-year-round home? Or are you looking for a long-stay holiday home? If the latter is the case, are you only considering you and your partner, or are younger family members involved in the decision too? It is easy to get carried away with rosy daydreams of regular visits from friends and family, and if you are not careful you may end up buying a villa that is far too large for your day-to-day needs. It may be preferable to start with a smaller property, especially if you have yet to make up your mind about future plans. For occasional holidays, grandchildren are quite happy with make-do beds and sleeping bags. Extra accommodation can probably be found locally for extra guests if it is absolutely necessary.

FINDING A PROPERTY

There are a number of sources of sound information which you can research when you are considering purchasing a property abroad. As with any new venture, you want to get yourself as informed as possible in order to participate fully in the process, ask the right questions or – alternatively – be in a position to consult the person who will ask the right questions!

There are interesting property and travel features in the Saturday issues of most of the quality daily newspapers, as well as in the quality Sunday press. These features often focus on the lesser-known parts of a country which are of interest to potential property buyers. In addition to newspapers, there are specialist magazines such as *International Property Homes*, *Homes Overseas* and *Homes Abroad*, which you can order from your newsagent.

Another good source are the regular exhibitions organised by property developers. Developers are also frequently represented at retirement exhibitions. Look out for advertisements for these events in both the national and local press.

Estate agents are another obvious source of information and many of the larger UK agents are now opening overseas departments for the sale of property abroad. The Royal Institution of Chartered Surveyors, to which many agents are affiliated, does not cover property abroad, but you should feel reasonably safe dealing with a long-established firm with a reputation to maintain.

Be wary of the short low-price inspection tours offered by overseas property developers and estate agents. They may provide a cheap trip and, if a purchase results, your money may be refunded. *But that should in no way influence your choice.* Be prepared to make more than one trip, under your own steam if necessary. See as much property as you can while you are in any one region; only by viewing can you make reasonable comparisons between what is available from different vendors. You are not inspecting just the properties, of course, but the immediate location, which is equally if not more important.

Before any decisions are made, consider carefully the resale potential of what you are buying. If the initial sale is through a UK estate agent, or via a local licensed agent with formal links with the UK, resale may be easier. It goes without saying that it can be difficult to sell on a recent development where sales are slow and new properties are still available.

BUYING PROPERTY ABROAD – SOME GENERAL GUIDELINES

The 'dos and don'ts' appearing below are the advice of a solicitor who specialises in foreign property, and who has written a series of booklets on the subject (see p 142).

- ◆ DO consult a British lawyer before you agree to anything.
  DON'T sign anything until you have consulted a lawyer.

- ◆ DO read the small print in any documents you are given.
  DON'T hand over any money until your lawyer tells you to.

- ◆ DO insist on a clause granting a 'cooling-off' period in any purchase agreement.
  DON'T let anyone talk you out of seeking all the professional advice you want.

- ◆ DO get all documents translated into English and insist and ensure that it is an accurate and full translation.
  DON'T make any irrevocable decisions until after you return home.

Procedures in property purchase vary from country to country, according to local regulations, and you need to seek out as much background information as you can on the country of your choice. The Allied Dunbar Money Guides are essential reading for anyone wishing to live in those countries (see p 142). Not only do the books cover property purchase, they also put into context the tax position and residency requirements of the countries concerned.

The Federation of Overseas Property Developers, Agents and Consultants (FOPDAC) publishes individual fact sheets which outline the legal procedures of property purchase in many different countries. They also produce a basic leaflet containing a checklist of questions which you should ask yourself before inspecting any property (see p 137).

Other sources of guidance include two self-help organisations, which can provide useful information. They are the International Property Owners Organisation (see p 137) and The Institute of Foreign Property Owners in Spain (see p 137). There are also membership clubs for property owners offering access to discounted flights, eg Owners' Club International and Intasun, Skyworld Villa and Appartment Owners' Club (see p 137).

— *John and Eileen Margerison* decided that when John retired at the age of 60, they would use some of their savings and accrued pension rights to buy a property on the Costa del Sol. They calculated that if they bought a small property to begin with, they could afford to keep on their house in the UK for perhaps two or three years, at which point they could decide where they wished to live permanently.

They decided to look for a two-bedroomed apartment in a price range of between £45-50,000. They obtained details of various properties from agents in both Spain and the UK, and decided to go and view a number of these independently. They both felt that if they went on an inspection flight, they would be unduly pressurised. Prior to leaving, they consulted a specialist solicitor, who advised them that, whatever the temptations, they should neither sign a contract nor pay a deposit on a property while they were away. They resolved to follow this advice even if it meant jeopardising the 'bargain of a lifetime', and planned to return to the UK for a 'cooling-off' period before making their final decision.

John and Eileen found a property they wanted to purchase within a few days. They successfully resisted pressure from the local estate agent and refused to sign any document until they returned to the UK.

On their return, they decided they wished to proceed with the purchase and contacted their solicitor accordingly. His first step was to get in touch with a solicitor in Spain who was an associate of his UK office. The Spanish solicitor then instigated local searches into the property in order to ensure that it had been built on an approved plot, that planning permission had been acquired, that there were no local by-law contraventions, and that the property was not subject to any outstanding tax or mortgage. (When you buy property in Spain, you are liable for all debts secured on the property whether you know about them or not.) In addition to all this, investigations were made on their behalf with regard to the public utilities (eg water, electricity, etc) and the value of the property for rating purposes.

John and Eileen were warned at this point that under no circumstances should they pursue the estate agent's suggestion to underdeclare the purchase price of the property in order to save themselves tax. Although the price of the property was the equivalent of £48,000, the agent suggested that they declare it as £38,000 in their *escritura* (the deed of conveyance), and thereby save themselves the tax on £10,000. The solicitor warned that this was illegal and, on discovery, would land them with an expensive fine.

Another suggestion made by the estate agent was that John and Eileen should pay the purchase money in pounds sterling because the vendor of the property was British and lived in the UK. They discussed this option with their advisors, who warned them of a financial technicality which might cause problems in the future. If they went ahead with the purchase, in sterling, and subsequently sold the property, they could have problems bringing their money back into the UK. This is because they would not be in possession of the appropriate bank certificates which normally endorse the importation of convertible pesetas into Spain to finance property purchase. In 1992 it is intended that there will be free movement of money throughout the EC; nevertheless, John and Eileen felt they would prefer to have the added protection of a bank certificate and decided to reject the estate agent's suggestion and pay the purchase price in pesetas.

When it was clear that all matters were in order, John and Eileen signed the contract and paid a deposit through their solicitor, who remitted it to Spain through the proper channels and obtained the proper receipts. As they did not wish to travel to Spain in order to sign the final documentation, John and Eileen gave Power of Attorney to the Spanish solicitor, which entitled her to sign the legal documents of transfer of the property on their behalf.

Two and a half months later, the completion date was set and John and Eileen were asked for the balance of the money, which again they paid through their solicitor. Their funds were despatched to Spain to the office of the Spanish associate who, in turn, arranged for the money to be transferred to the vendor's solicitors. The *escritura* was signed that same day and the keys to the property were made available. John and Eileen were then notified that the property belonged to them.

Arrangements were then made for the *escritura* to be registered with the authorities, a process which takes about three months, after which time it would be made available to John and Eileen.

All in all, the purchase took about four months from the day of actually viewing the property to the final completion. John and Eileen could feel assured that a thoroughly professional job had been done on their behalf, and that they need have no worries regarding the property in the future.

Although this story has a happy ending, there were a couple of 'danger points' in the transaction where things could have gone badly wrong. The advice of a specialist solicitor enabled John and Eileen to make the right decisions. The most essential rule in buying property abroad is to seek independent professional advice. This costs money and it must be budgeted for. It is a necessity, not a luxury to be added on if you can afford it. You can't *not* afford it. When things go wrong with property purchase, it is nearly always because buyers have failed to take proper advice. No one advised by a lawyer, for example, would be likely to buy property on an unauthorised or illegal development, because lawyers know the proper enquiries to make.

Due to the many complaints received by the European Parliament about difficulties in the purchase of property abroad, particularly in Spain and Portugal, the European Parliament recently called for a special EC law to set minimum provisions covering basic consumer rights in property transactions abroad within the European Community.

There is a first time for everything. Remember how you once had to be guided through the procedures of house-buying in the UK? It is a different process abroad, but only seems more complicated because it is unfamiliar. Professional advice is vital, and it is important that this advice is independent. Be wary of developers who say their lawyers have checked everything. You need a lawyer who is acting for you – the buyer, not the vendor – who puts your interests first. There are UK firms who specialise in foreign purchase and a list of addresses can be obtained from the Law Society (see p 138).

GARDENS ABROAD

Once you have purchased your home in the sun, you may find yourself responsible for an area of garden or terrace. Gardening under Mediterranean conditions will present quite different challenges from those in the UK. The following advice is intended as a helpful start.

The balconies of modern apartments often have built-in troughs or window boxes, sometimes with their own irrigation system, and these are ideal for bright geraniums and trailing plants. Most familiar herbs like rosemary, thyme, sage, bay and basil originated in Mediterranean countries and can be grown in individual pots and containers.

At ground level, gardening is a matter of using plants – particularly climbers – in order to enhance areas like a patio, where you will be sitting out. Scented plants are wonderful in the evening. Plants may also be chosen to provide shelter from the sun or wind; vines are commonly used for this purpose.

If you are moving to sunnier parts, forget all about the green lawns and well-filled herbaceous borders of the English garden. Stone-paved surfaces with the occasional, strategically placed shrub, tree, or decorative pot are appropriate now. Scale and proportion will need practice as you get used to the rapid rate at which things grow! Whatever shrubs and plants you eventually choose will have to withstand long periods of drought during the summer months. You may like to think about collecting rainwater or recycling bath water. Water is likely to be metered, remember.

A Simple Guide to Gardening on the Costa del Sol from the Club de Jardinería de la Costa del Sol has been specially written to help newcomers to the Mediterranean start a garden. The book includes notes on the planting and care of suitable plants, and an English/Spanish vocabulary of gardening terms and plant names. It is obtainable from the Royal Horticultural Society (see p 138).

Other options

RETIREMENT HOMES AND SHELTERED SCHEMES

Retirement homes and sheltered apartments are a comparatively new venture on the Continent, although they are well established in places like Florida. Many private developers in the UK are now turning to Europe to benefit from the new market of the affluent elderly in France, Spain and Portugal. Among the buyers of these retirement/leisure apartments are older British expatriates who are already living abroad or, perhaps, leaving Hong Kong and South Africa. For these people, a place in the sun is a more attractive alternative than returning to the less pleasant climate of the UK. Advantages for residents of these luxury apartments include:

- Freedom from worry about decorating and maintenance. In addition, apartments are often furnished or part-furnished.

- Garden upkeep is guaranteed, although there may well be individual window boxes for you to look after, if you wish.

- Security is provided by the presence of a resident manager (usually English-speaking), an alarm system and/or an entryphone.

- Facilities can include a bar or clubroom, a swimming pool and/or gymnasium, chiropody and hairdressing services and sometimes a weekly health clinic.

Although the cost of these retirement apartments may seem cheap compared with UK prices for sheltered accommodation, the maintenance and service costs are considerably higher. As well as additional costs for relative basics like air conditioning and swimming-pool maintenance, you are probably going to end up paying for facilities you may not use.

It is hard to make generalisations because such developments as there are abroad tend to vary. However, there are lessons to be learned from the experience of residents in similar schemes in the UK, which – it has to be said – have not always proved to be very popular or successful. Often, there are disadvantages which are not obvious at the outset. Living exclusively with a group of people who are all of one age does not work for everyone. It can make a lot of people *feel* old. Residents sometimes complain of 'living in a ghetto' or, alternatively, of 'living in a goldfish bowl' – a reference to the gossip between members of predominantly female, rather cliquey groups of residents.

Problems with fellow-residents are a hazard of moving into this kind of environment. When looking over an apartment, it would be wise to meet other occupants. Alternatively, some schemes which run these apartments along 'club' lines check out the compatability of new applicants by means of a diplomatic interview with founder members. Neither strategy is a guarantee of future good relationships with fellow residents. There is another factor involved here. Often, a bad choice of location increases the dependency on other residents for companionship. Some retirement apartments in the UK have been built on unsuitable, perhaps hilly, sites, a long way from shops and other community facilities. This increases a sense of isolation and cuts off residents from opportunities to meet and make friends with people beyond their immediate environment. Location matters a great deal, especially as you get older and find it more of an effort to get out and about.

Another drawback experienced by UK buyers of retirement accommodation has been annual service charges which can sometimes increase by more than the rate of inflation. These are subject to legal limits in some European countries.

Many people feel, however, that buying sheltered housing has been the best move they have ever made. The advantages they mention include not having to worry about major repairs, knowing that there is 24-hour emergency cover and having other people around whilst still being able to enjoy complete privacy.

Before considering this type of property purchase, it may be worth reading *A Buyer's Guide to Sheltered Housing*, published by Age Concern England and the National Housing and Town Planning Council (NHTPC). Although this publication does not deal with property abroad, it does give you an idea of what is involved in the design and management of retirement accommodation. One point emphasised in this booklet is that the quality of the management services has a far greater influence on the happiness and comfort of the residents than do any amount of luxury fixtures and fittings. While the developer of a sheltered housing scheme may be a well-known British building firm, this is no guarantee of the management company, and no safeguard against a future takeover or buy-out. The Guide advises prospective purchasers of what they can expect as a result of the House Building Council's Code of Practice on management and services in private sheltered housing.

Buying into one of these schemes might be a good idea if you are already living abroad. However, in other circumstances it could be a little late in the day to be venturing so far from home. Over the age of 70 or thereabouts, you may well prefer living in the UK, and taking holidays abroad in the winter. That way you get the best of both worlds.

TIMESHARE

A lot of people's first introduction to timeshare is an encounter with the highly-pressurised sales tactics practised by some developers. A typical approach is via a letter, telling you that your name has been selected by computer as being eligible to receive a major award. To claim the award you must attend a special exhibition on 'holiday ownership', 'vacation ownership' or 'holidays for life' – all of which mean timeshare. People who go along often find themselves unpleasantly pressurised into signing an agreement there and then, without the opportunity to study the sales literature properly. The best place for such 'invitations' is the bin. There are better ways to find out more about timeshare.

Another common approach is a face-to-face invitation in a resort abroad. Holidaymakers are invited to view apartments, where refreshments are included in the tour. A heady mix of the carefree holiday mood and a few glasses of wine can make heavy persuasion hard to resist. *Never* be in a hurry to make important and irreversible decisions in this way. If you are told that this great offer cannot wait until next week, then you can be sure it is no great offer in the first place. *Your Place in the Sun* is a leaflet from the Department of Trade and Industry (see p 143) which alerts prospective sunseekers to the dangers of this 'quick-sign, halfprice' kind of salesmanship, which – although bad practice – is not against the law.

So, what is timeshare? Timeshare is a compromise; a property purchase without a lot of the headaches which come with owning a holiday home. What you are purchasing is a stake in a holiday property abroad, for your exclusive use during a set period each year usually a week or a fortnight. It may be yours for a specified number of years to come or in perpetuity. The cost will depend on a number of things: the degree of luxury of the resort, the variety and type of amenities and, most significantly, the time of year. Retired people are able to take holidays at off-peak times and should benefit from favourable rates, but check that it isn't the rainy season first!

Timeshare owners have the reassurance that 'their' property is occupied and well maintained in their absence. There is an annual maintenance charge which usually covers repairs and decoration, local rates and taxes, utilities like gas, water and electricity, maid service and laundry, and a management fee. There should also be a sinking fund for any major work which may be required. The maintenance charge is worked out as a weekly charge, which increases in line with local inflation and is adjusted annually. Multiplying the weekly service charge by 50, to arrive at the annual figure, will give an indication of how reasonable (or otherwise) this cost is at the outset. As a buyer on a retirement income, you will need to consider whether these annual costs are within the budget you would wish to allocate for holidays.

In addition, you have to pay for your flight and upkeep. Some resorts have arrangements for reduced air fares and car hire, but make sure you check on the all-year-round availability of these.

With timeshare you are making a decision which affects holidays for years ahead. A capital outlay is involved and, although this amount can be paid over a number of years, your money remains tied up. It is therefore important to consider and compare the cost benefit of what you are buying in order to be sure that it really suits your circumstances. Any cost comparisons you make should be with a hotel of similar standards, but ask yourself whether such standards are really important to you.

Timeshare should never be regarded as an investment. Resale within five years is not recommended and is almost certain to result in a loss. Selling at a profit at any time cannot be guaranteed. Indeed, it is not always easy to sell at all, so if you are thinking of purchasing a timeshare, it may be worth looking out for a 'buy-back' guarantee which is offered by certain sales companies.

With timeshare, you are not necessarily restricted to holidaying in the same resort year after year. Exchanges are possible for a fee, providing your timeshare organisation belongs to one of two worldwide exchange networks: Resort Condominiums International or Interval International (see pp 137-8). Similarly, if you are not able to make use of your slice of timeshare one year, the property may be lent to friends or relatives, or you may rent it out to strangers, either by private arrangement, or through an agency.

Further practical information can be obtained from the Timeshare Developers' Association (see p 143), a self-regulatory body, with a code of ethics on how timeshare should be sold. They produce a free leaflet called *Buying Timeshare You Can Trust*. As with all property purchase, legal advice is vital. Any resort affiliated to the Association will have clear contracts which have been vetted by a panel of independent specialist lawyers, but you may still like to consult your own solicitor. Most timeshare can be transferred or bequeathed in your Will.

— **Bill and Mary Llewellyn** bought a two-week slice of timeshare in a villa on Tenerife four years ago, while they were there on holiday. They enjoy their spell of 'summer' each winter, but the experience has not been without drawbacks, as Mary explains. 'Timeshare brings back memories of pressure-selling at its worst, which – even in retrospect – I still find objectionable. Make no mistake, it is a hard sell. What was on offer was highly eyecatching accommodation, beautifully furnished. The whole place was beautifully laid out: the gardens with all the flowers, the heated swimming pool and so on. We were vulnerable – and fell. Had there been the three-day 'cooling-off' period on offer, when you have time to think, I am certain we'd have backed down.

'I don't think we would do it again, simply because it is unnecessary to make such an expensive commitment. However, we have been back to Tenerife three times and are looking forward to the fourth. We enjoy what is our villa for two heavenly weeks of summer in February. And in years to come I know our three daughters – each with their own family – will be able to enjoy it too.'

Take your time with timeshare. It is a buyers' market and there is absolutely no need to hurry. Don't rush into the first scheme that comes your way. Have a good look around; the character of a resort can change dramatically due to overdevelopment. A final thought: timeshare units have very high marketing costs. If you are attracted to the idea of timeshare, then buying somewhere 'secondhand' in a mature resort, where all new building has ceased, could result in a bargain.

Further Information

USEFUL ADDRESSES

HOLIDAY OPTIONS

Camping and Caravanning Club (CCC)
11 Lower Grosvenor Place
London SW1W OEY
Tel: 01-828 1012

Canada, Australia, New Zealand, United States, Parents and Associates (CANUSPA)
National Secretary
Mr T Selwood
24 Florida Court
Reading
Berkshire RG1 6NX
Tel: 0734 574757

Canvas Holidays
Bull Plain
Hertford
Hertfordshire SG14 1DY
Tel: 0992 553535

Central Bureau for Educational Visits and Exchanges
Seymour Mews House
Seymour Mews
London W1H 9PE
Tel: 01-486 5101

Christians Abroad
1 Stockwell Green
London SW9 9HP
Tel: 01-737 7811

***En Famille* Overseas**
The Old Stables
60b Maltravers Street
Arundel
West Sussex BN18 9BG
Tel: 0903 883266

Eurocamp Travel Ltd
Edmundson House
Tatton Street
Knutsford
Cheshire WA16 6BG
Tel: 0565 3844

Gîtes de France
178 Piccadilly
London W1V 9DB
Tel: 01-493 3480

Global Home Exchange
c/o Mrs Jay Newling
12 Brookway
Blackheath
London SE3 9BJ
Tel: 01-852 1439

Home Interchange
8 Hillside
Farningham
Kent DA4 0DD
Tel: 0322 864527

Interhome
383 Richmond Road
Twickenham
Middlesex TW1 2EF
Tel: 01-891 1294

Intervac Home Exchange
6 Siddals Lane
Allestree
Derby DE3 2DY
Tel: 0332 558931

Lion World Travel Ltd
Friendship House
49/59 Gresham Road
Staines
Middlesex TW18 2BD
Tel: 0784 465511

Portland Holidays
218 Great Portland Street
London W1N 5HG
Tel: 01-388 5111
or
1 Portland Street
Manchester M1 3BJ
Tel: 061-236 9966

Saga Holidays plc
Middelburg Square
Folkestone
Kent CT20 1AZ
Tel: 0800-300 456 (free)

Travel Companions
89 Hillfield Court
Belsize Avenue
London NW3 4BE
Tel: 01-431 1984/01-202 8478

University of the Third Age
(U3A)
National Office
c/o BASSAC
13 Stockwell Road
London SW9 9AU
Tel: 01-737 2541

Weider Travel
The Strand Cruise Centre
Charing Cross Shopping
Concourse
Adelaide Street
London WC2N 4HZ
Tel: 01-836 6363

Youth Hostels Association (YHA)
Trevelyan House
8 St Stephen's Hill
St Albans
Hertfordshire AL1 2DY
Tel: 0727 55215

OTHER SOURCES OF HELP AND ADVICE

AA Travel Services
PO Box 100
Halesowen
West Midlands B63 3BT
Tel: 021-501 7805

Airpets Oceanic
Spout Lane North
Stanwell Moor
Staines
Middlesex TW19 6BW
Tel: 0753 685571

Air Travel Advisory Bureau
320 Regent Street
London W1R 5AB
Tel: 01-636 5000

Association of British Travel Agents (ABTA)
55-57 Newman Street
London W1P 4AH
Tel: 01-637 2444

British Airways Medical Services for Travellers Abroad
7 Bury Place
London WC1A 2LA
Tel: 01-831 5333
(recorded information service)

British Airways Travel Clinics
PO Box 10
Heathrow Airport
Hounslow
Middlesex TW6 2JA

British Association of Removers (BAR)
3 Churchill Court
58 Station Road
North Harrow
Middlesex HA2 7SA
Tel: 01-861 3331

BBC Video World
Subscription Service
PO Box 177
Basingstoke
Hampshire RG24 OFG
Tel: 0800 444141

BBC World Service
Bush House
London WC2B 4PH

British Council
10 Spring Gardens
London SW1 2BN
Tel: 01-930 8466

British Diabetic Association
10 Queen Anne Street
London W1M OBD
Tel: 01-323 1531

British Executive Service Overseas (BESO)
Mountbarrow House
12 Elizabeth Street
London SW1W 9RB
Tel: 01-730 0022

British Insurance Investment Brokers Association (BIIBA)
   14 Bevis Marks
   London EC3A 7NT
   Tel: 01-623 9043

Civil Aviation Authority (CAA)
   ATOL Section
   45-59 Kingsway
   London WC2B 6TE
   Tel: 01-832 5620

Department of Social Security (DSS)
   Overseas Branch
   Central Office
   Benton Park Road
   Newcastle-upon-Tyne NE98 1YX
   Tel: 091-285 7111

Fernox Britannica Works
   Clavering
   Essex CB11 4QZ
   Tel: 0799 550811

Federation of Overseas Property Developers, Agents and Consultants (FOPDAC)
   PO Box 981
   Brighton
   Sussex BN2 2FT
   Tel: 0273 777647

General Register Office
   (Births, Deaths and Marriages)
   St Catherine's House
   10 Kingsway
   London WC2B 6JP
   Tel: 01-242 0262

Holiday Care Service
   2 Old Bank Chambers
   Station Road
   Horley
   Surrey RH6 9HW
   Tel: 0293 774535

Inland Revenue
   Public Enquiry Room
   West Wing, Somerset House
   Strand
   London WC2R 1LB
   Tel: 01-438 6420

Instituto de Propietarios Extranjeros SA
   (Institute of Foreign Property Owners in Spain)
   38 Hillfield Road
   West Hampstead
   London NW6 1PZ
   Tel: 01-431 2499

Intasun, Skyworld Villa & Apartment Owners Club
   Intasun House
   2 Cromwell Avenue
   Bromley
   Kent BR2 9AQ
   Tel: 01-466 4244

International Property Owners Organisation
   72 Tottenham Court Road
   London W1P 9AP
   Tel: 01-323 1225

Interval International
   Agriculture House
   25-31 Knightsbridge
   London SW1X 7LY
   Tel: 01-823 1666

Law Society
   50 Chancery Lane
   London WC2A 1SX
   Tel: 01-242 1222

London Regional Transport (LRT)
   Unit for Disabled Passengers
   55 Broadway
   London SW1H OBD
   Tel: 01-222 5600

Medical Advisory Services for Travellers Abroad (MASTA)
   London School of Hygiene and Tropical Medicine
   Keppel Street
   London WC1E 7HT
   Tel: 01-631 4408

Medic-Alert Foundation
   17 Bridge Wharf
   156 Caledonian Road
   London N1 9UU
   Tel: 01-833 3034

Overseas Settlement Board for Social Responsibility
   Church House
   Dean's Yard
   London SW1P 3NZ
   Tel: 01-222 9011

Owners' Club International
   Centurion House
   Bircherley Street
   Hertford SG14 1BH
   Tel: 0992 554511

Oyez Law Stationers
   49 Bedford Row
   London WC1R 4LS
   Tel: 01-242 7132

Resort Condominiums International
   Parnell House
   19 Wilton Road
   London SW1V 1LW
   Tel: 0536 310111

Royal Automobile Club (RAC)
   49 Pall Mall
   London SW1Y 5JG
   Tel: 01-839 7050

Royal Association for Disability and Rehabilitation (RADAR)
   25 Mortimer Street
   London W1N 8AB
   Tel: 01-637 5400

Royal Horticultural Society Enterprizes Ltd
   RHS Gardens
   Wisley
   Woking
   Surrey GU23 6QB
   Tel: 0483 211320

Solitaire
   PO Box 2, Hockley
   Essex S55 4QR

Travel Advice Unit
Consular Department of the Foreign and Commonwealth Office
Clive House, Room 635
Petty France
London SW1H 9HD
Tel: 01-270 4129

Woman's Corona Society
Commonwealth House
18 Northumberland Avenue
London WC2N 5BJ
Tel: 01-839 7908

CONSULATES

Australian High Commission
Australia House
Strand
London WC2B 4LA
Tel: 01-379 4334

Austrian Embassy & Consular Section
18 Belgrave Mews West
London SW1X 8HU
Tel: 01-235 3731

Belgian Consulate General
103 Eaton Square
London SW1W 9AB
Tel: 01-235 4414

Canadian High Commission
38 Grosvenor Street
London W1X 0AA
Tel: 01-409 2071

Cyprus High Commission
93 Park Street
London W1Y 4ET
Tel: 01-499 8272

French Consulate General
21 Cromwell Road
London SW7 2DQ
Tel: 01-581 5292

New Visa Section
PO Box 57
68 Cromwell Place
London SW7 2EW
Tel: 01-823 9555

Greek Consulate General
1A Holland Park
London W11 3TP
Tel: 01-727 8040

Italian Consulate General
38 Eaton Place
London SW1X 8AN
Tel: 01-235 9371

Malta High Commission
16 Kensington Square
London W8 5HH
Tel: 01-938 1712

Netherlands Embassy
38 Hyde Park Gate
London SW7 5DP
Tel: 01-584 5040

New Zealand High Commission
New Zealand House
80 Haymarket
London SW1Y 4TQ
Tel: 01-930 8422

Portuguese Consulate General
62 Brompton Road
London SW3 1BJ
Tel: 01-581 3598

Spanish Consulate
20 Draycott Place
London SW3 2RZ
Tel: 01-581 5921

Swiss Embassy
16 Montagu Place
London W1A 2BQ
Tel: 01-723 0701

USA Embassy
(visa enquiries)
5 Upper Grosvenor Street
London W1A 2GB
Tel: 01-499 3443

Yugoslav Embassy
7 Lexham Gardens
London W8 5JJ
Tel: 01-370 6105

NATIONAL TOURIST OFFICES

Australian Tourist Commission
Gemini House
10-18 Putney Hill
London SW15 6AA
Tel: 01-780 1424

Austrian Tourist Office
30 St George Street
London W1R OAL
Tel: 01-629 0461

Belgian National Tourist Office
Premier House
2 Gayton Road
Harrow
Middlesex HA1 2XU
Tel: 01-861 3300

Tourism Canada
Canada House
Trafalgar Square
London SW1Y 5BJ
Tel: 01-629 9492

Cyprus Tourist Office
213 Regent Street
London W1R 8DA
Tel: 01-734 9822

French Government Tourist Office
178 Piccadilly
London W1
Tel: 01-491 7622

Gibraltar Tourist Office
179 Strand
London WC2R 1EH
Tel: 01-240 6611

Greek National Tourist Organisation
4 Conduit Street
London W1R ODJ
Tel: 01-734 5997

Italian Tourist Office
1 Princes Street
London W1R 8AY
Tel: 01-408 1254

Malta Tourist Office
207 College House
Suite 207
Wrights Lane
London W8 5SH
Tel: 01-938 1140

Netherlands Tourist Board
25-28 Buckingham Gate
London SW1E 6LD
Tel: 01-630 0451

New Zealand TP Travel
New Zealand House
80 Haymarket
London SW1Y 4TQ
Tel: 01-930 8422

Portuguese National Tourist Office
New Bond Street House
1-5 New Bond Street
London W1Y ONP
Tel: 01-493 3873

Spanish National Tourist Office
57 St James Street
London SW1A 1LD
Tel: 01-499 0901

Swiss National Tourist Office
Swiss Centre
New Coventry Street
London W1V 8WE
Tel: 01-734 1921

USA Travel and Tourism Administration
32 Sackville Street
London W1X 2EA
Tel: 01-439 7433

Yugoslav National Tourist Office
143 Regent Street
London W1A 8RE
Tel: 01-734 5243

RECOMMENDED READING

BOOKS AND MAGAZINES

Allied Dunbar, *Your Home in France, Your Home in Italy, Your Home in Portugal*, second edition 1989, *Your Home in Spain*, second edition 1989 (Longman).

Allied Dunbar, *Expatriate Tax and Investment Guide*, third edition (Longman, 1989).

Bennett, T, *A Guide to Buying a Property in Portugal, A Guide to Buying a Property in Spain, A Guide to Buying a Property in France*. Available from Russell & Russell, 9-13 Wood Street, Bolton, BL1 1EE.

Consumer Association, *Holiday Which?* Available to *Which?* subscribers. Details from Consumer Association, FREEPOST, Hertford SG14 1YB.

Consumer Association, *Renting and Letting: the Legal Rights and Duties of Landlords and Tenants*, (Hodder & Stoughton, 1989).

Dawood, Dr R, *How to Stay Healthy Abroad*, second edition (Oxford University Press, 1989).

Disability Alliance ERA, *Disability Rights Handbook*. Available from 25 Denmark Street, London WC2H BNJ (15th edition due April 1990).

Employment Conditions Abroad, *Outlines for Expatriates*. Available for 70 countries from Anchor House, 15 Britten Street, London SW3 3TY.

Financial Times, *Resident Abroad*, Financial Times Magazine for Expatriates. Available from Subscription Department, Central House, 27 Park Street, Croydon CR0 1YD.

Financial Times, *Retiring Abroad*. Available from Financial Times Business Information, 7th Floor, 50-64 Broadway, London SW1H 0DB.

Furnell, M, *Living and Retiring Abroad: The Daily Telegraph Guide*, third edition (Kogan Page, 1989).

Guardian Publications Ltd, *Guardian Weekly*. Available to subscribers from Guardian Publications Ltd, 164 Deansgate, Manchester M60 2RR.

Homefinders Publications, *Buying Overseas Property, A Guide to Buying Property in France, A Guide to Buying Property in Portugal, A Guide to Buying Property in Spain. Homes Overseas, Homes Abroad* (monthly magazines available from large newsagents). All available from 387 City Road, London EC1V 1NA.

Lees, D and M, *Travel in Retirement*, (Christopher Helm, 1989).

Outward Bound Newspapers Ltd, *Australasian News, Canada News* and *South Africa News*. Available from 1 Commercial Road, Eastbourne, East Sussex BN1 3XG.

LEAFLETS

British Telecom, *Phoning the UK from Abroad*. Available from your district office or, to order, by dialling 100, asking the operator for Freephone BTI, (Mon-Fri 8.00 am-10.00 pm).

Department for Social Security (DSS), *SA 29 Your Social Security, Health Care and Pension Rights in the European Community, SA 40 Before you go, SA 41 While you're away, NI 38 Social Security Abroad*. All available at your local office.

Department for Trade and Industry (DTI), *Your Place in the Sun*. Available from Consumer Affairs Division, DTI, 10-18 Victoria Street, London SW1H ONN.

Inland Revenue, *IR 20 Residents' and Non-residents' Liability to Tax in the UK*. Available from Inland Revenue, Public Enquiry Room, Somerset House, Strand, London WC2R 1LB.

Office of Fair Trading, *Holiday Travel*. Available from Office of Fair Trading, Field House, 15-25 Bream's Buildings, London EC4A 1PR.

Timeshare Developers' Association, *Buying Timeshare you can Trust*. Available from Timeshare Developers' Association, 23 Buckingham Gate, London SW1 8LB.

OTHER PUBLICATIONS FROM AGE CONCERN

A wide range of titles are published under the Age Concern imprint.

GENERAL

Living, Loving and Ageing
Sexual and Personal Relationships in Later Life
Wendy Greengross and Sally Greengross

Sexuality is often regarded as the preserve of the younger generation. At last, here is a book for the older person which tackles the issues in a straightforward fashion, avoiding preconceptions and bias.

£4.95   0-86242-070-9

Famous Ways to Grow Old
Philip Bristow

A collection of letters from a host of internationally distinguished figures, outlining their personal attitudes to the onset of old age. Full of amusing and touching anecdotal material. Contributors include: James Callaghan; Peggy Ashcroft; Cardinal Basil Hume and Barbara Cartland.

£8.95   0-86242-087-3

Grandparents' Rights
Jill Manthorpe and Celia Atherton
Co-published with the Family Rights Group

In today's society, with the everchanging pattern of family relationships, many grandparents have become separated from their grandchildren. This book details their legal position and provides practical help and advice on how to approach these emotional crises.

£3.95   0-86242-079-2

Loneliness: How to overcome it
Val Marriott and Terry Timblick

Loneliness can affect us all at some point in our lives, as the letters from celebrities featured in this book demonstrate. Here is a source of practical advice on ways in which to relieve such isolation co-written by one of the country's leading advice columnists.

£3.95   0-86242-077-6

HOUSING

A Buyer's Guide to Sheltered Housing
Co-published with the NHTPC

Buying a flat or bungalow in a sheltered scheme? This guide provides vital information on the running costs, location, design and management of schemes to help you make an informed decision.

£2.50   0-86242-063-6

HEALTH

The Magic of Movement
Laura Mitchell

Full of encouragement, this book by TV personality Laura Mitchell is for those who are finding everyday activities more difficult. Includes gentle exercises to tone up muscles and ideas to make you more independent and avoid boredom.

£3.95   0-86242-076-8

The Foot Care Book: An A-Z of fitter feet
Judith Kemp SRCh

A self-help guide for older people on routine foot care, this book includes an A-Z of problems, information on adapting and choosing shoes and a guide to who's who in foot care.

£2.95   0-86242-066-0

MONEY MATTERS

Your Rights
Sally West

A highly acclaimed annual guide to the State benefits available to older people. Contains current information on income support, housing benefit and retirement pensions, among other matters, and includes advice on how to claim them.

£1.50   0-86242-080-6

Your Taxes and Savings
John Burke and Sally West

The complexities of our tax system as it affects those over retirement age are explained in straightforward terms in this invaluable annual guide. Advice is given on how to complete your tax return, how to avoid paying more tax than necessary and how to make the most of your money.

£2.70   0-86242-081-4

Using Your Home as Capital
Cecil Hinton

This best selling book for home-owners, which is updated annually, gives a detailed explanation of how to capitalise on the value of your home and obtain a regular additional income.

£2.50   0-86242-084-9

If you would like to order any of these titles please write to:
Age Concern (DEPT LS1)
Freepost
Bernard Sunley House
Mitcham
Surrey CR4 9AS

We hope you found this book useful. If so, perhaps you would like to receive further information about Age Concern or help us do more for elderly people.

Dear Age Concern
Please send me the details I've ticked below:

other publications ☐   *Age Concern special offers* ☐

volunteer with a local group ☐   *regular giving* ☐

covenant ☐   *legacy* ☐

Meantime, here is a gift of

£ _____   PO/CHEQUE or VISA/ACCESS No _____

NAME (BLOCK CAPITALS) _____

SIGNATURE _____

ADDRESS _____

_____ POSTCODE _____

Please pull out this page and send it to: **Age Concern** (DEPT LS1)
FREEPOST
Mitcham,
no stamp needed **Surrey CR4 9AS**

ABOUT AGE CONCERN

Age Concern England, the publisher of this book as well as a wide range of others, provides training, information and research for use by retired people and those who work with them. It is a registered charity dependent on public support for the continuation of its work.

The three other national Age Concern organisations – Scotland, Wales and Northern Ireland – together with Age Concern England, form a network of over 1,400 independent local UK groups serving the needs of older people, assisted by well over 250,000 volunteers. The wide range of services provided includes advice and information, day care, visiting services, voluntary transport schemes, clubs and specialist facilities for physically and mentally frail older people.

Age Concern England
Bernard Sunley House
60 Pitcairn Road
Mitcham
Surrey CR4 3LL
Tel: 01-640 5431

Age Concern Scotland
54A Fountainbridge
Edinburgh
EH3 9PT
Tel: 031-228 5656

Age Concern Wales
4th Floor
1 Cathedral Road
Cardiff CF1 9SD
Tel: 0222 371821/371566

Age Concern Northern Ireland
6 Lower Crescent
Belfast
BT7 1NR
Tel: 0232 245729

ABOUT THE TSB

The sunnier climates frequently found abroad are extremely popular with British people after they have reached retirement age. And why not? After a lifetime of work you may well feel that you deserve a place in the sun.

Some choose to live permanently away from Great Britain while others opt for a holiday home in which to spend a few months each year. Perhaps you too are contemplating such a move?

If you are, financial considerations may be uppermost in your mind so why not browse through the following pages and see just how simple money matters can be, courtesy of TSB. The following is just a summary of TSB's major financial services designed to make life easier and more convenient for you, whether you are holidaying or living abroad.

MONEY AND TRAVEL

Before you go on holiday have you thought about *Travel Insurance?* A policy from TSB will protect you against most unforeseen circumstances such as medical expenses and loss of baggage and the cost of such a policy is very competitive.

The next consideration that you'll need to make is *Foreign Currency.* Traveller's cheques are much safer than carrying large amounts of cash, although it's a good idea to have some foreign currency at hand as well for tips, refreshments, transport and incidentals when you arrive at your destination. All TSB branches can supply you with traveller's cheques and the popular foreign currencies.

If you have a *TSB Cheque Account* you can also benefit from *TSB Eurocheques*. These are accompanied by a eurocheque card and work just like a cheque book and card in Britain. The card guarantees your cheques up to the approximate local equivalent value of £100 and you simply complete the cheque in local currency. The amount will be debited automatically from your TSB Cheque Account.

A credit card is another convenient means of making payments abroad and here the *TSB Trustcard* can help you. It's valid at every outlet displaying the VISA sign (there are more than six million worldwide) and with it you can also obtain cash in local currency from VISA banks and VISA cash dispensers.

LIVING ABROAD AND BANKING BY PHONE

Telephone banking is with us and available to all. Undoubtedly the most sophisticated advance in personal banking for several years, it has made many daily transactions more convenient – simpler too – than ever. And when you live abroad but maintain a bank account in Britain the benefits are even greater.

The *TSB Speedlink* telephone banking service gives you direct access to your TSB Cheque Account. With a simple telephone call, 24 hours a day, you can transfer funds from one account to another, pay bills, obtain an up-to-date balance or request a statement.

3-IN-1 CONVENIENCE WITH BANKCARD ABROAD

Another highly useful aid to managing your money abroad is the *TSB Bankcard*. This is really three cards in one: a debit card for use at VISA outlets, a cheque guarantee card and a Speedbank card for withdrawing cash from VISA cash dispensers.

As a debit card the TSB Bankcard is a lot more convenient than paying by cheque as all you have to do when paying for goods or services is present your card. The cost of your purchase will be debited automatically from your TSB Cheque Account so you're no longer restricted by the limit usually imposed on cheque guarantee cards. You can use it wherever you see the VISA sign. If you'd rather use a cheque there's nothing to stop you, provided of course that you are writing cheques in the UK or Channel Islands, and the TSB Bankcard serves as a cheque guarantee card too.

As a Speedbank card it's ideal. Use it at any VISA cash dispenser and withdraw cash in local currency up to the equivalent of £200 per day. Other than that, the only limit on the amount that you can draw is the balance in your TSB Cheque Account.

BANKING SERVICES FOR THE EXPATRIATE

TSB Overseas Branch (TSB Channel Islands Limited) has a wide range of services available to customers living abroad. As well as TSB Bankcard and Speedlink there's an *Offshore* Premium Account, designed specifically for expatriates, that pays a high rate of interest gross on a quarterly basis. The minimum balance required is £2,000. A cheque book, TSB Bankcard, eurocheques and Speedlink are all available with this account and there are no restrictions on deposits or withdrawals.

Fixed Term Deposits can be arranged on balances in excess of £5,000 and interest rates can be quoted for periods of one month to three years. Subsequent deposits are normally reinvested with your capital plus interest for a further similar term and, if you wish, the interest can be paid into another TSB account.

Foreign Currency Accounts can also be arranged for Two Day Call and Fixed Term Deposits with your cash converted into US dollars or other foreign currencies. The rate of interest offered will concur with the current market rate ruling in the currency of your choice.

In addition TSB Channel Islands offers *Portfolio Management* and a comprehensive *Stock Exchange Securities dealing service*, together with a *Computerised Expatriate Advisory Service* that will be of particular value to you if you're planning to live or work abroad.

The latter is a fully personalised service requiring you to fill in a questionnaire that enables the Bank to offer help with financial planning before you move.

Taxation, social security and the general implications of moving abroad can be covered by this extremely useful service.

OTHER SERVICES

Current Accounts
7 Day Deposit Account

GENERAL

Interest paid on deposits held with the TSB Bank in the Channel Islands is paid gross, without the deduction of any tax at source. It will, however, be encumbent upon yourself to make the necessary declarations to the relevant Revenue Authorities and we recommend you contact your tax advisor in this respect.

TSB Channel Islands Limited has its principle place of business in Jersey, Channel Islands. The paid up capital and reserves exceed £41 million, as at 31st October 1988. Deposits made with the offices of TSB Channel Islands Limited in the Channel Islands are not covered by the Deposit Protection Scheme under the Banking Act 1987 as the Channel Islands are not part of the United Kingdom.

Copies of the most recent audited accounts are available on demand.

For further information contact your local TSB branch or telephone Freephone 0800 289670.